GW01066143

How to Analyze People

*The Complete Guide to Reading Body
Language and Nonverbal
Communication. Learn Emotional
Intelligence Skills to Speed Read People*

Robert Eastman

Table of Contents

Introduction

Congratulations on purchasing *How to Analyze People: The Complete Guide to Read Nonverbal Communication, Apply Emotional Intelligence, and Detect Lying.* We thank you for doing so! You've taken the next step in your evolutionary development.

You should know that you're not alone, and there's nothing wrong with you for wanting more confidence and control over the interactions you have in your daily life. There are a great many individuals around the world that also face the challenge of learning to train yourself to read and communicate in a deliberate and strategic way.

You're on the verge of learning fundamental functions of positive, deliberate communication and influence, which can get you the outcome you want in nearly any situation; social, business, or romantic. Not only will you learn about the basics of human behavior and what drives us to react the way we do, but you'll also learn how to adjust your own body language broadcasting in a way that will benefit you.

As you move through the following chapters, you'll become familiar with what inherent behaviors and natural factors drive us. You'll learn how to identify informational personality types and learn how to use this to emphasize your position. You'll get a sense of how the subconscious mind works and how you can use this to your benefit in an influential situation.

As you learn to use these tools, you'll be introduced to over a dozen techniques and exercises you can practice, to train your mind to think and act deliberately in your benefit. The practices of persuasive body language and vocal language play an important role in the techniques and exercises you'll learn. With this information, you'll gain an understanding of the origins of these practices and how to apply them to your own goals.

In just seven chapters, you'll have gained confidence and control over your own interactions, and you'll be prepared for what exercises to practice and master in order to maintain positive momentum.

Chapter 1: Nonverbal Communication

It's not what you say, and it's not how you say it. It's both. Scholars indicate that most people use nonverbal communication to formulate the majority of opinion about someone else. Some indications even claim that upwards of 60 percent of communication takes place non-verbally. Other professionals will argue and claim that no such measurement has been made in a reasonably accurate way that takes into account the various forms of written communication in the modern-day world, like texting, social media posts and comments, emails, and chats.

So where is this communication coming from, if not from our words and language? It's being broadcast by the body in movements, posture, expressions, gestures, and other nonverbal sounds. Even silence is revealing communication. These messages are being broadcast by us and received by us at almost imperceptible rates. In fact, a facial expression can be made and interpreted in less than 1/16th of a second. Therefore, deliberate or not, hundreds of thousands of years of social training have given us the inherent skills to send and receive nonverbal communication in a highly efficient and effective way.

With so much of our communication being done nonverbally, it's important to ask yourself just how much you're actually paying attention to. How much are you missing?

If you were able to pick up more information about someone and their intentions just by knowing what to look and listen for, how much different could your social interactions be?

If you possess the understanding of all of the typical (and not so typical) signs of nonverbal communication, you could understand people better, you could influence the conversation more easily, and you could spot when deception is afoot. Better, even, perhaps, is the ability to conduct yourself and present yourself in a way that communicates exactly what you want others to pick up on, either consciously or unconsciously.

The information in the following chapters will help you to expand your knowledge of, and reach with, the power of reading others and the power of deliberate communication, both verbally and nonverbally. Whether this is your introduction to it, or you've been practicing for a while, the foundational information in these chapters serves as a refreshing review and a crash course in analyzing others to benefit you in all of your interactions, may they be based in love, business, or family, or otherwise.

Understanding these concepts will level the playing field. It will likely even put you at an advantage. Body language communication happens naturally in any social situation, and it can be applied in a deliberate way to any interaction.

It doesn't matter how much money you earn, how you earn it, how old you are, or what sex and race you identify with. Anyone who understands these basic skills can use them. In fact, you'll begin to see that many of us are already using these tactics, but in largely subconscious ways, such as in marketing and sales. Many, too, are broadcasting themselves without a deliberate thought about it; unaware of the detriment and harm it could be done.

So now it's up to you. You can continue to trip and stumble along down the same path you've been going, or you can learn how to analyze the verbal and nonverbal information surrounding you every day. You can learn how to use related techniques deliberately to gain the results you want from any social interaction.

Defining Nonverbal Communication

To begin, let's refresh ourselves on what nonverbal communication is and how it works. When we think of communication, typically the first thing we think of is speaking. Speaking is definitely an important way for us to communicate, but most of the communication is going on around the words being said. The words actually account for very little. Communication is the act of sending or receiving information between two or more individuals, and this is not always spoken. By communicating, we're able to share knowledge, lessons, and skills. This information is shared in two major ways: verbally and nonverbally.

Nonverbal communication, then, is quite simply all the kinds of communication we conduct without words. This includes actions that are both happening at a conscious and an unconscious or subconscious level. This might be the clothes worn by the communicator or the posture with which he or she stands. It might be facial expressions and gestures. There's even nonverbal communication present within verbal communication, such as unspoken communications like the speaker's tone, pitch, cadence, volume, timbre, register, or even their silence. Every little piece of information which is not directly said is nonverbal communication.

Where you might be able to control and even stop yourself from what you say, most nonverbal behaviors are largely involuntary and thus quite revealing. It is only when we study the art of deliberate communication that we begin to gain control over those largely involuntary behaviors.

It's critical to understand that most of a person's opinion of you is derived from the nonverbal communications you broadcast. The words you speak have very little to do with what someone thinks of you. If you've been rehearsing a speech over and over in order not to mix up your words, you should consider how much more beneficial that practice time would be to make adjustments and controls to the nonverbal cues you're sending.

When an individual says one thing, but their body says another, the audience picks up on this, either consciously or subconsciously. Impressions, opinions, and decisions are made based on this information. If the visual or physical doesn't seem to match the verbal, we instinctively recognize that something is amiss.

In various studies, scholars agree that the very words you use in your speaking make up only about 5% of someone's opinion of you. The nonverbal voice cues you're sending will make up for about 45% of an opinion of you, while a whopping 50% of the opinion consists of your nonverbal body language communication.

Keep in mind that this is an approximate measurement for face-to-face interaction. Written communication operates a bit differently, and while writing, communication does incorporate many of the same nonverbal elements, it must be observed and measured separately.

With so much of an opinion being formed on communications other than our words, it doesn't seem so strange to spend more time practicing the nonverbal parts of your speech, than the words themselves.

Nonverbal Communication: Then and Now

It was only in the 1870s when we began to question nonverbal communication in any significant or scientific way. The idea of nonverbal communication was raised with the publication of Charles Darwin's third major work, *The Expression of Emotions in Man and Animals*. It was in Darwin's observation of nonverbal communication between animals that it was considered among humans. Today, the study continues and expands. Understanding and using nonverbal communication today is more than scientific observation; it's a profession. There are many professions that bank on their nonverbal communications to lead the way and set the profile.

When it comes to guiding and inspiring other professionals, knowing a thing or two about nonverbal communication makes all the difference. Keynote speakers take the stage to inspire sales teams. Trainers and coaches hold students accountable for reaching the goals they've set. Whether to inspire a sales team, a singer, an actor, an athlete, a parent, or a student with important exams, coaches are always working with the patterns of thought and behavior exhibited by their clients.

Not only does Tony Robbins attest to deliberately using deliberate nonverbal communication on himself, and within business and social situations, he teaches others how to do the same. Tony Robbins is a very well-known American author and life coach who regularly hosts or speaks at seminars that cater to a wide variety of individuals. The audience is often comprised of business professionals, entrepreneurs, and other driven individuals wanting to accelerate their success and develop themselves on a professional or personal level. He speaks on the theory, the how-to, and the virtues and results of a lifestyle augmented by the ability to read individuals and communicate in an influential way.

Robbins, along with many other coaches and speakers at a local or national scale, teaches individuals how to use verbal and nonverbal language and behavior to assess and therefore influence interactions. Learning the art of reading and broadcasting both verbal and nonverbal communication puts you at an advantage, allowing you to command an audience with confidence.

It allows you to say just the right, impressive, things at the right time for that romantic or financial prospect. It allows you to move more freely through a host of social situations you'll inevitably find yourself in at some point, or regularly.

For coaches that guide sales teams and entertainers, teaching others to project themselves deliberately is one of the primary functions. So much of what we do is a psychological game more than anything else. No matter if you speak to a king, a saint, or degenerate, the inherent senses that emotion plays upon is an equalizer. We are all human. We all want safety, food, and shelter. We all desire to be of value and to be loved. We all strive for self-actualization.

The art of analyzing others acknowledges this and utilizes it to elicit a particular response from the individual or the public. The desired response comes as a result of the harmony between the language of the actual body and language.

Name another professional that distinctly adheres to the philosophies of deliberate body language and verbal language — attorneys and lawyers; especially trial lawyers. Trial lawyers routinely represent clients in significant court cases, arguing in their client's support and defense. Without a doubt, this requires a keen sense of how one conducts himself in the courtroom. It requires a deliberate intention to build a conscious and subconscious rapport with the jury and judge. A trial lawyer must also guide the client him or herself in the deliberate body language and deliberate speech for the best possible results in the trial.

Nonverbal and verbal persuasion is used to build a rapport with the judge and jury. It's important to be able to read the body language of the jury in the initial stages. It provides insight to the lawyer about which areas of the trial of the story need more attention, emphasis, or avoidance.

The way a juror might fold their arms, rest their posture, or the micro-expressions on their faces, all provide an indication of the mental and emotional workings of that individual at the time. In addition to reading the body language of the individual jurors, the lawyer must know what's needed to broadcast themselves as sure, confident, and authoritative. This is not done by facts and words alone, but by the way in which one carries him or herself, the way in which one conducts himself or herself on the courtroom floor. All of these factors are weighed by the jury, either consciously or subconsciously.

The lawyer assesses the jury and their nonverbal communications to make a determination about the best way to tell the story. The lawyer can then change the tone, cadence, volume, timbre, and register of voice during certain points throughout the trial, to add influence and persuasion.

Without the skills to read the body language and expressions of the jury, the judge, the witness, the opposing party, and the client, there would be little control over persuading the jury. Without these skills, the lawyer would not be able to serve better, the client in defending his or her rights. Reading the nonverbal communications of others, and broadcasting your own nonverbal communications deliberately, are both fundamental tools for this profession.

In the business world, the role of a negotiator is to ensure that maximum value is felt by each counterpart. To achieve this, negotiators must read, interpret, and communicate in a deliberate and tactful way. In most cases, a rapport has been developed, and it's at this sometimes-stressful point that the relationship is most fragile. The wrong phrasing or timing and the rapport which has been built could collapse. The negotiation could go sour and result in an indefinite delay or a withdrawal of interest. To avoid this, negotiators employ a series of tactics to maintain the interest of their counterparts and to demonstrate high value.

One of the primary ways to read and influence your prospect is to actually listen to what your prospect is saying, both in their language and in their body. If you listen carefully, instead of just waiting for your next chance to say something brilliant, you'll actually pick up on clues and tidbits of information that you can use later with your prospect to persuade them.

An example of this might be a sales professional trying to close one of the biggest sales so far. In an attempt to demonstrate value, the sales professional prepares a PowerPoint presentation of all the major features and functionality that will surely impress the prospect. However, when the sales professional listens to the prospect closely and carefully, it becomes clear that the prospect is only concerned about one major aspect: customer service. The sales professional could go one of two ways.

If careful listening has been applied, the sales professional will realize the PowerPoint presentation of features and functionality they've prepared is virtually useless. Just the prospect wants to trust that the sales professional will be responsive and supportive. The skilled negotiator with focus on this. If the professional has *not* listened carefully, the plan is probably still to try and dazzle the prospect with the PowerPoint presentation of features, which will ultimately lose the interest of the prospect instead.

Another fundamental skill of a masterful influence in any interaction is to come prepared if possible. If you're headed to a job interview, do your homework first. Look up the company's website online. Get familiar with it. What topics were recently covered in the company blog? What services are provided, and at what cost? We can see how the ability to read body language and other nonverbal cues play a large part in negotiation. These are only a few of the fine professions that make a living reading the communications that others are broadcasting. The success that these individuals experience can be the success you experience from your own application of these tools.

Types of Nonverbal Communication

With so much information packed into nonverbal communication, it's probably not a surprise that there are many forms of it. These very common behaviors below fall into three main groups.

The face communicates very often through:

- Eye contact
- Eyebrow movement
- Smiling
- Fake smiles
- Lips
- Wrinkling the nose
- Facial expressions

Facial expression is the main way we communicate emotions without the use of any words or noises. Facial expressions are universal in nearly every case. No matter where you go, you'll see the same facial expressions to convey emotions of surprise, fear, disgust, anger, sadness, and happiness. You may notice that facial expressions are very often used in conjunction with other verbal speech and nonverbal behaviors in order to make as clear a display of emotion as possible. This is evident in the dramatic example of theatre actors and the like using exaggerated expressions, body language, and gesticulation, in order to make it clear to the audience what the character is feeling - and better yet, what the character wants other characters to *think* he feels.

The body communicates very often, though:

- Hand gestures
- Posture
- Body orientation
- Body language
- Space and distance, or proximity
- Touch
- Personal Appearance
- First impressions

The perceptions others have about you is largely drawn from how you hold and carry yourself. Body language and body movement, give others ideas about you, whether they are conscious or unconscious of decoding this information. This could be the posture you keep when you walk in the room, when you stand to speak, when you cross the street, and when you meet someone for the first time. Consider your clothing and appearance and the extension of body language. Surveys indicate that most people judge an individual based on their appearance in less than 3 seconds. Among the most popular elements judged first are the shoes someone wears, the hairstyle (including facial hairstyle) someone chooses, the clothing they wear, and the hands, including nails.

Paralinguistic communication very often consists of:

- Humor
- Silence
- Symbolism
- Sarcasm
- Tone
- Volume
- Pitch

Paralinguistic are bits of information communicated with sound, and with the vocal cords in particular, without actually being words. This could be a gasp of fear, a sigh of relaxation and contentment, or a groan when a terrible smell is encountered. This also can include using elements of conversation subtly, such as humor and sarcasm. This could also be the myriad ways an individual uses the voice while communicating words. When a speaker changes pitch and tone, there is a recognizable change in the decoding of that information. When a speaker speaks loudly and then whispers, it elicits a different response from the audience in each case.

Shaking Hands

Another component of body language which is often overlooked, but truly deserves its own attention, is the handshake. Unlike facial expressions, the etiquette and expectations of a handshake can vary from region to region. Some handshakes are fast, and some are slow. Some are aggressive, and others are soft. Some deliberately impose a subconscious signal to assert dominance, and others seek to show compassion and ultimate respect. Some handshakes should not be made unless the two individuals are of the same gender. In still other cases, the handshake can be seen as cold and callous, where a closer greeting such as hugging or kissing, might be more appropriate.

But all of these examples, under analysis, are revealing critical information to you. Whether for personal reasons or socially imposed ones, some information can be derived that hints to whether the person feels confident or shy; entitled or unworthy.

Handshakes as a social behavior seem to go back at least to the 5th century BC and have been depicted as communication of greeting, congratulations, and particularly, agreement. In almost every case, the handshake is taking on the whole to symbolize honesty and respect between the two individuals. We see this in sports, politics, business, and in customs like shaking the hand of a newly married groom.

In some parts of the world:

- Men are more likely to shake hands than women
- It's appropriate to shake a woman's hand before a man's
- Children shake hands when meeting
- A firm shake is rude

- A kiss is part of the shake
- Both hands are used
- A soft shake is a sign of respect
- The handshake is held during the entire conversation

All over the world, in communities where handshakes are expected, there are individuals who do not want to shake hands, and furthermore, are afraid to shake hands. In some respects, this makes sense, as the fear comes from that of contamination and not necessarily connecting via touch. Some individuals, though, do not physically like the way it feels to touch others. For whatever reason, someone has, they may not want to shake hands. In many cultures, this has been taken as a sign of disrespect, and certainly there are still many regions that observe it as such, but in the modern world, and especially in cultures where business and commerce takes precedence, we become more accepting of skipping the shake and bonding and building rapport in new ways. Sometimes we might see this as the elbow bump (and similar shared gestures like it), which seems to be an acceptable compromise somewhere between making contact and not making skin contact.

Another part of the handshake that is often overlooked is the eye contact that goes with it. In most cases, you should make appropriate eye contact with the individual when you shake their hand. A handshake that includes eye contact conveys honesty and truth. Likewise, a handshake that includes one or both individuals avoiding eye contact is a sign of mistrust and deception. Keep in mind that both the handshake and eye contact, could be getting encoded deliberately, but then, pay attention to signs of deception and lying.

Next, we'll take a closer look at how parts of the Limbic system and the mind affects the way we react and respond.

Chapter 2: The Roles of the Mind

There are several ways in which the mind plays a role in how we behave, and in turn, how we interpret that behavior. In this section, we'll take a look at the significant role of the limbic system and emotion on our human behavior, as well as the role of the subconscious mind. By the end of this section, you should have a solid understanding of the components in the mind that influences us, and what the mind is thinking when it's encoding and decoding information.

Encoding and Decoding

When we talk about broadcasting and receiving information from others in verbal and nonverbal ways, we're really talking about the process of encoding and decoding. When you encode information, you're generating it. This could be a smile, a sigh, or folding your arms in front of you. When we're observing the transmission of encoded information, we interpret that information and call it decoding.

There are a number of factors that play a part in how we encode and decode information, especially social information. For example, a hand gesture in one part of the world can be positive and friendly, but that same hand gesture can be exactly the opposite in another part of the world.

The Limbic System

The limbic system is an easy way to refer to and describe several interconnected parts of the brain, all of which play a large part in our emotions and self-preservation. Though most of these components of the brain are more or less considered to be a part of the limbic system, it depends on who you ask. Some professionals include five brain components in their interpretation of the limbic system, while others include eight or more components of the brain to make up the limbic system. It's in the limbic system that you can find triggers for memory, motivation, addiction, and survival. It's thought to be one of the longest developed parts of a mammalian brain, but still, we know so little about it. Senses, especially the sense of smell, is highly associated with this part of the brain. The limbic system, then, is often referred to as the "feeling and reacting" brain, and this is how we too will think of it.

Let's take a look at some of the most widely accepted components that make up the limbic system. Though these components are interconnected and work together, they are all responsible for different aspects of our responses and emotions.

Hypothalamus

The hypothalamus is involved in sexual function, endocrine function, behavioral function, and the nervous system. The hypothalamus is connected with the frontal lobes, septal nuclei and the brain stem reticular formation by way of the medial forebrain bundle. It receives input from the hippocampus by way of the fornix and the amygdala. Some functions that require direct input from environmental stimuli take place in this region of the brain, such as the regulation of body temperature, endocrine functions, appetite, and again, sex.

Amygdala

The amygdala makes connections with many brain regions, including the thalamus, hypothalamus, septal nuclei, orbital frontal cortex, cingulate gyrus, hippocampus, parahippocampal gyrus, and brain stem. The amygdala is critically involved in managing behavioral responses and responses related to the endocrine and nervous systems. This is where we see responses such as revenge and rage, fear, and anxiety.

Hippocampus

The hippocampus is an ancient area of the brain. It helps to control corticosteroid production but is also significant in processing and understanding spatial relations within the environment. The hippocampus is also largely responsible for memory functions. It's the hippocampus that decodes information, stores it, and retrieves it.

Limbic Cortex

The prefrontal cortex is crucial for judgment, insight, motivation, and mood. It's also related to the function of reacting in a conditioned way. When an individual suffers

Damage to the prefrontal area, there are difficulties with abstract thinking, judgment, moods, and critical thinking skills. The prefrontal cortex is also strongly influenced by the use of alcohol. When an individual suffers a mood disorder or dysfunction, it's in the prefrontal cortex that abnormality is often found.

All of these functions focus around instinct and emotion and therefore make up a significant part of how we respond to stimuli and how we interpret responses to stimuli. If these areas of the brain have experienced trauma or damage, then the chances are more likely that this will become clear by careful attention to the individual's behaviors and responses.

The Conscious, Subconscious, and Unconscious Mind

Since you'll be referring to the subconscious mind moving forward with the art of influence, it will help to refresh what you know about brainwave functionality. As you may be aware, human beings exhibit several brainwave functions on a daily basis. As an individual wakes from sleep and begins to perform the morning regimen, the brainwave functionality continues to change. On the way to work and throughout the day, the individual passes through multiple phases of brainwave functionality. The flow from one brainwave function the next is a natural occurrence that happens to all human beings, all the time. We normally shift from one to the other as if we're moving through a scale. The scale moves from beta brainwaves to alpha waves, then to theta brainwaves.

Beta brainwaves can be thought of in comparison to the critical mind; concentrating, ever-assessing, and making decisions based upon stimuli. Alpha brainwaves are closer to that magic spot; the subconscious mind. In this state, you find yourself relaxing. This is probably your brainwave functionality as you're watching a movie or even reading this book. This is generally a state of calm where the imagination is allowed to unfold. The magic spot is really in the theta brainwaves. You've probably been in the theta state at least once in the last 24 hours if you've been asleep. If you've ever been hypnotized, you've experienced the theta state. If you've ever found yourself lucid dreaming, you've been in the theta state.

There is another brainwave functionality - so-called delta waves. If you've gone too far, you're in delta mode. That's okay; it's an excellent result. Delta mode is what's happening when you experience REM sleep.

As someone who wants to ignite your prospect's imagination, you're aiming for something between the alpha state and the beta state, but it can definitely depend on the person and the circumstance. For example, you're definitely not going to be able to lull a sales prospect or a romantic interest into a hypnotic trance in order to influence them on the spot, so you'll need tactics that are built for the subconscious but interact on a conscious, logical, level.

The individual's protector and decision-maker is the conscious mind, the beta brainwave machine. This is the critical thinking, logical, mind that constantly surveys its surroundings and catalog data. This is the mind that is learning and concentrating and keeping us safe and comfortable from the day's stimuli.

Imagine you're driving down the road to a place you've been hundreds of times. It's almost as if your hands- as if your car itself, knows the way automatically. You know the way to go so automatically that your mind begins to wander.

You think about what you should have said to that person the other day, or what tasks are waiting for you at home. This is your mind in the alpha brainwave mode, but of course, the beta mind is still focused on safely driving the road it knows. Before long, you look around, and you're halfway there, and you don't even remember the first part of the drive.

You continue leisurely along in alpha mode, winding the route you know so well you don't even need to think about it, and in an instant-- a deer runs out in front of your car. Your beta mind engages immediately, responding to the sudden stimuli and reacting fast enough to slow and swerve and miss the deer; alpha thoughts left swiftly behind.

The conscious analytical mind and beta brainwave function are critical for survival, but it's not the most conducive for making effective suggestions because the analytical mind will latch onto the data to filter and sift and compare against what it knows already. The critical mind could essentially talk you out of any deliberate suggestion before it even gets planted in the subconscious mind where it can begin to take hold. You might tell yourself consciously that you're going to finally close this big client by the end of the month, but your critical mind will be quick to point out:

- The client is probably considering other options
- You haven't closed a deal this big ever
- You haven't closed them yet
- The client has a tendency to drag their feet

- Even the top salesperson at your company hasn't closed a deal this large

As many scenarios as the conscious mind can think of to guard against, it will. In doing so, it kills any hopeful thought before it takes root. Contrary to how it sounds, the conscious mind is not doing this to harm you but to help you. It's weighing as much information as it can to make sure you're safe and comfortable.

If the conscious mind thinks that a loss of income on this deal is a safety concern, it will do all it can to guard against that, including act like you will not be getting it. Instead of acting upon a healthy seed you could have planted in the subconscious mind, the body acts in accordance with what the critical mind says.

The subconscious mind is a state of mind and not necessarily a place in the brain. The subconscious mind is a reference to a frame of mind between conscious, aware thought, and unconsciousness. The imagination "lives" (for lack of a better term) within the subconscious mind.

One of the most crucial pieces of being a good influence is understanding a key function of the subconscious mind. It believes what it's told. The subconscious mind doesn't know the difference between fantasy and reality; it just believes the story, it's told and acts in accordance with that story.

What this means for you, positive persuader is that if you keep feeding yourself negative stories about losing and staying down, your subconscious mind believes this. It acts in accordance with this belief, finding evidence of this around you and shouting for your attention: "You were right, you'll never be confident! You were right. These people don't respect you! You were right. You have no control over this!" What's more, it's not only your subconscious that acts in accordance with these thoughts you continue to repeat. Your body begins to obey these thoughts, as well. Soon, mentally and physically, you're living the same negative story you've been repeating in self-talk and out loud to others.

But this isn't bad news. If the mind believes what it's told, then you can tell it positive and beneficial ideas and stories. Your subconscious mind and your body will begin to respond to and act in accordance with those ideas instead.

To illustrate more clearly, think of a book or a movie you've read or watched that has such a sad or touching moment that you actually end up crying or feeling emotional. Your logical, conscious mind knows it's only a movie or a story. This is why you don't actually run and hide during the scary scenes. This is why you don't actually call 911 for help when a character gets hurt. It's your logical mind that determines the experience is just a story and not a real circumstance for you to manage.

The subconscious mind is different. It does not distinguish between the movie and the real-life circumstance. The subconscious mind only cares about the story and the emotions and characters involved. So, when you come to the part of the story that brings you to tears, this is the work of the subconscious mind. The subconscious mind believes the story that is being told and starts to produce emotions and feelings to accompany the story.

Though the subconscious mind believes the stories you tell it, especially in the alpha or theta states, you cannot easily go against someone's core belief structure, or it will be disruptive and cause the critical mind to re-engage. This would pull a person from an alpha-theta state into a beta state pretty quickly.

Your subconscious mind is an imaginary genius. It becomes so engaged in the emotion and the story that it prompts your body to respond to these emotions physiologically. The body literally begins to cry because the subconscious mind is experiencing sadness, despite the sadness not being real. Using the subconscious mind is a critical skill for the skilled reader of others and the influence of interactions.

The unconscious mind is a bit of a mystery to psychology, but as we continue to explore, we find the unconscious mind to be wider and deeper than we could have expected. Comprehensive studies have been conducted, and evidence gathered to suggest the unconscious mind is where we store instincts and automatic reactions, as well as hidden phobias and desires. It's also suggested that the unconscious mind is where we hold repressed feelings and psychological complexes. It is in the unconscious mind where subliminal perception takes place.

The concept of the unconscious mind has become a part of our language and culture through the famous works of psychoanalysis, Sigmund Freud, and Carl Jung. Jung, and especially Freud, would frequently tap into the unconscious minds of patients by analyzing dreams and forgotten memories. You're likely familiar with "the Freudian slip," which is another revealing act of the unconscious. A Freudian slip is a slip of the tongue that reveals, unconsciously, your true feelings about a subject. This usually comes out as a word you didn't mean to say, instead of the word you tried to say.

The unconscious mind is also the resting place for trillions of bits of information collected throughout a lifetime and organized into a pattern. To organize patterns, the mind groups information into stories. It's suggested that by putting information into the form of a story, complete with emotion, the brain is able to process and store a higher concentration of information. Humans have an inherent need to organize information in story form, consciously, and unconsciously. If we know the mind in all of its forms is strong with organizing a story format, then we, as influencers and persuaders, can use this information.

When you want to get the point across, try telling it as a story and see if this is a more effective method for getting at your audience with emotion. The subconscious mind willingly follows the storyline and believes what it's told, so be sure to plan deliberately, what your message will convey.

Human Behavior

It's important to acknowledge the primary drives for our inherent human behavior. The human may be a complex creature, but we are driven largely by a surprisingly few basic instincts.

We're all equipped with basic human behaviors that help us to process and manage the environment around us. They help us to survive and adapt. When we react to internal and external stimuli, it's often with a demonstration of one of the following instinctual behaviors:

Denial is a very common coping mechanism is denial. When we're confronted with a situation that doesn't feel good or is overwhelming, one of the first things we do is deny it. We pretend it's not happening or that it doesn't exist, even though the problem or situation is very real. This can range from the relatively inconsequential to the severe. For example, you may be faced with a task you don't like doing, or that you don't feel confident doing. Instead of dealing with the task, you may consciously or subconsciously procrastinate on the task or forget to do it altogether. In a more drastic example, an individual could be faced with the stark truth that a loved family member has passed. Rather than accept that truth, the individual might deny it. The individual may continue to talk about the loved one and act as if they haven't passed; as if they're still here. Denial may not be the healthiest coping skill, but it is one most of us share and commonly use, whether we mean to or not.

We feel a commitment to our tribe, partly because we want our tribe to be loyal to us, but also because it's in our best interests to stay on good terms with the tribe. Staying on good terms with the tribe is a relatively easy way to ensure shelter, food, safety, and a sense of belonging. Depending on the stimulus, we react by either displaying loyalty or asking for it. In either case, loyalty is an instinctual behavior mostly used for selfish reasons of self-preservation, rather than altruism as it might initially seem.

Regardless, the idea of loyalty has built just as strong an entertainment following as revenge. We see allegiance and loyalty expressed in various ways all around us. Families demand loyalty, as do sports teams. To go against the group and turn your back on family, or a football team, would not be a socially acceptable move. Not only would the group have issues letting you back into their arms, but other groups will catch wind of your disloyalty and question whether you should be included.

Loyalty to the company we work for is expected. Loyalty to brands, loyalty cards, it's an undeniably popular theme. We want loyalty from others, and we want to be perceived as loyal in order to maintain a respectable position within the social group.

Revenge is one of the most interesting behavioral instincts we exhibit. For ages, humans have reacted with the desire for personal justice when we are confronted with a stimulus that we perceive as trespass against us. We don't just want to be righted. We want to punish the wrong-doer. We don't want a random person to suffer the punishment. We want the one who has done wrong to suffer the consequences.

Seeing revenge is a little bit like an addict seeking a fix. It is likened in our brains to the equivalent of a shot of dopamine or serotonin. Just the idea of getting revenge excites the part of our brain responsible for processing reward. Getting a taste of revenge is, at least at first, like a chemical boost of dopamine or serotonin. Revenge is used often as a drive for movies and stories because it's so strong and so relatable to us. Almost anyone you know has wanted revenge at one time or another.

We think revenge will make us feel better, but that can sometimes backfire. When we get revenge, sometimes it turns out that the feeling of satisfaction is short-lived and the revenge is not as expected. In many cases, a feeling of sinking to the same level as the wrong-doer makes us feel worse. Worse yet, the constant thinking about deserving revenge and getting revenge, and the thoughts about having taken revenge, all make for a fresh and open wound that will not be allowed to close and heal. We're under the impression that revenge will be a sense of closure for us, but we often find the opposite is true in the end.

If revenge is so deeply a part of us, forgiveness must be, too. The power of forgiveness is an important part of revenge to also be aware of in your social interactions. Sometimes the power derived from acting in forgiveness and empathy is greater than anything we could hope for with revenge.

Greed is an instinct that's a bit harder to define and measure. We tend to display greed in circumstances where we are convinced; we will not have enough. This could be money, food, anything really. In reaction to a stimulus, we may end up hoarding these things in an attempt to protect ourselves. Another reason we tend to display greed when confronted with a stimulus is due to a psychological function referred to as a superiority complex. This is when you want something someone else has, and you don't want them to have it so that you can appear to be the superior individual with the covetous property.

Finally, perhaps the most obvious and the most powerful is the desire for procreation.

The last of the major instincts that drive us is the inevitable and deep-seated need to produce offspring. It's perhaps no surprise that the strongest instinct we are driven by being the instinct that has continued to keep our species alive. Without this powerful drive, we may not be here now. It's easy to understand then why this instinct rooted solely in producing a bloodline to surpass us is the one that controls a large part of how we react to those stimuli. Sex, attraction, romance: these are the tools of an influencer looking for love, or at least physical copulation. Our drive for sex is so powerful that we've come to a point in evolution where the desire for the sexual interaction surpasses the root need to create offspring.

It's important in many societies to present yourself as a candidate for sex. This is expressed in a number of ways and varies depending on the culture, but it's very common in each distinct culture to follow the social norms of someone who is either eligible for mating or already paired with another. This can, in some cultures, come as a particular hairstyle, headdress, or clothing to wear. In some cases, the jewelry or the markings on one's body will inform others in the tribe of the individual's status as a sexual partner.

In the United States, sex has morphed into a set of industries that aim to make a profit off of this instinctual drive. The clothing industry, makeup industry, even the car industry all bank on our innate need to establish ourselves as viable sexual options. The pharmaceutical industry even plays their hand at either helping us to conceive or guards us against conceiving.

The entertainment industry tells us what the social norms are for sexy, and we mirror these traits or try to, in order to increase our odds of a sexual relationship of some kind. Whether our instinct drives us to want to reproduce truly, or whether the drive is more about an appearance or a status, you'll find the need for sex is a powerful tool that can offer a great deal of leverage in just about any interaction you'll have.

Genetics are the characteristics we inherit from our parents can certainly play a role in how we process, manage, and react to stimuli and confrontation. Though we do not all share the same genetics, we do share the same experience that genetics play a part in our human behavior. Hereditary characteristics may be visible or not. This could be exhibited as visual trait-like freckles, dimples, and hair color. It might also manifest as a subconscious behavior like teeth-grinding, or even an unseen illness like hypoglycemia.

As we've evolved into a species that prefers to live and work in communities and groups, we've developed sets of social norms. These are the basic rules of the society that tells us how to think and behave to fit in with the group. There are four main types of social norms that can be found in a typical group or community. Traditions are customs and beliefs passed down from generation to generation, generally about, what is right and wrong. Mores are the moral and ethical standards that the group or community observe and use for a compass. Taboos are the behaviors that the group or community deems unacceptable; those who conduct themselves in an unacceptable way are often shamed or removed from the group. Laws are the official rules set by a group or community; members of the tribe are expected to obey these rules or suffer the consequences; these rules are usually enforced by the tribe's government.

Another factor that drives us is an opportunity for creativity. We want to be free to express ourselves and be of value to those around us by using our creative skills. When we are given tasks or jobs that allow us to solve problems creatively and encourage us to think creatively, we perform better, nearly every time.

We don't get burnt out as easily or quickly, and we take pride in our work. People are driven by creativity, and this is one reason that creative programs inside of businesses like Google and Amazon are so successful. Employees are given a regular opportunity to express themselves creatively to solve a problem or develop something, or constructor design something with regularity each month. They dedicate 10% of their work time each month to follow the creative streak on anything they want. Everyone feels valued, and they feel the satisfaction of using their own creativity to accomplish tasks.

All of these instincts and factors play a role in the ways we react. Now that you know what it is that causes us to react so strongly, you can use this information to read interactions, elicit positive responses, or mitigate negative reactions.

Chapter 3: Emotional Intelligence Skills

So far, we've gained a solid understanding of what is meant by nonverbal and verbal communications and reviewed examples of nonverbal communication. If you're analyzing others or expecting others to examine you, then realizing how significant these communication cues make an impact is critical. As much as half of an individual's opinion of you is based on nonverbal communications.

We've also taken a look at other factors in the mind that cause us to encode and decode information in the ways we do. This includes the limbic system, the subconscious mind, and inherent human behaviors like revenge. Next, we'll take a look at understanding emotional intelligence and how it plays a part in your becoming a master of the art, reading others, and being read.

Emotional intelligence, also known as EI, is putting all of this information together into a skill set that allows you to register and manage the emotions within yourself and the emotions of others in your environment. When an individual demonstrates a high capacity for emotional intelligence, they show the ability to know what emotions are being felt by themselves and others, what those emotions mean, and how those emotions will impact others in the environment.

Studies suggest (but are also classically refuted) that a high capacity for emotional intelligence is a crucial trait of being a leader. To think of this in even a rudimentary and common-sense way, it makes sense. The person to lead and manage others is the person who best understands how everybody's personality types will work together. The person to lead is the one that stays calm and not the person who loses his or her cool in a moment of stress. It's a little more than that, though; a strong leader would demonstrate a keen grasp on specifically five points of emotional intelligence:

- Self-awareness
- Self-regulation
- Motivation
- Empathy
- Social Skills

If an individual demonstrates a strong understanding of their own emotions at most times, and the individual has a sense of how those emotions affect others in the environment or community. Being self-aware typically also means being able to identify your own strengths and weaknesses.

Self-regulation is basically a way of saying an individual doesn't think or act impulsively. There are typically no rushed decisions made, and while the individual may hold personal emotions about a circumstance is stimuli, he or she also understands that there is a more significant benefit to considering all feelings and positions, not just one's own opinions and position. Therefore, the individual doesn't react based solely on the information inside oneself, knowing full well that there are other pieces to consider.

Motivation, in this case, refers to the individual's ability to stay motivated oneself, and also to encourage others. The individual has the ability to inspire self and others to action, to keep self and others motivated with the task at hand, especially when the going gets tough. The motivated individual will see the team over the finish line.

The individual who shows empathy is someone who can put themselves in someone else's shoes. This is also most probably the individual who considers what's best for everyone in the environment or community, and the person who offers constructive criticism, for self and others. This individual is a deliberate listener of both verbal and nonverbal cues in order to gather the most information about a situation or topic.

The individual with a high capacity for understanding and using social skills is generally someone with excellent communication skills. This individual wants to get the most comprehensive information available and will take the bad news just to get the good news, too. The motivator is often also the communicator, as it takes a refined knowledge of communication to do it in a way that guides or leads a team or community to success. These are the individuals who can support their team and get everyone excited about a new goal. Those with excellent social skills are usually the ones who are able to manage tough situations and resolve them in the fairest and beneficial way.

The individual with a firm grasp of self-awareness, self-regulation, motivation, empathy, and social skills is often the one we find leading groups and communities. These are usually the types of individuals that rise to positions of power and guidance; teaching others to better themselves, their neighbors, or their environment. When an individual does not have a firm grasp of these concepts, it's incredibly challenging to make it to such a position or to retain that position for an extended period of time.

Understanding of and attention to these emotional intelligence skills puts you ahead of the pack in a number of other ways as well. Studies have revealed that a higher EI-score was indicative of such benefits as better health, better relationships, and better performance on nearly any type of task. Though the measurement of such a study has been challenged in more recent years, correlations still exist in a number of studies to suggest there is some relation to a grasp of emotional intelligence skills and how that shapes the path an individual might walk.

Leadership

For example, one study suggests that when it comes to jobs that are high-profile or require strong leadership, a firm demonstration of high capacity, emotional intelligence was twice as important as expertise or IQ.

A leader doesn't lead to words or experiences. A leader leads because of an acute awareness of who follows.

Can you recall a time you were given the responsibility of leading a group in some way, but you had no idea what you were doing? Instead of focusing on those around you and analyzing what you could from them, you may have panicked and tried to become an overnight expert on the problem or issue. You may have put a good deal of focus and time into making sure you understood every detail of the problem and every word you'd say if asked about it. You may have even attempted to organize some plan for resolution. But take that to the team, and also the best studying and most beautiful presentation of your plan aren't going to stand up for long. Because there's something you didn't give your time and focus to, and that was the analysis of your team. This is a classic mistake for individuals who are unaware of how to read people and use that information to advantage.

The individual who is practiced in the art of the analysis of others, being put into this sudden leadership position rather blindly would be no issue. Imagine again, being put in that position, but this time, imagine that you aren't worried one bit. You keep your cool and regulate your breathing. You will remain cognizant of the nonverbal communications coming from you. When you have your balance, you take inventory of the same in the members of your team, and you start to put together a picture of the entire scenario, not the problem. You already know there is a problem, and you have a general understanding of what it is and what the goal is. You also notice that the members of your team also know this. As you listen, you notice that each member of the team has a valuable idea about how to bridge the gap between the problem and the solution. As you listen, you get a sense of how worried everyone is about this problem, how confident they are about fixing it, what the risks and rewards will be. As you listen, you get a sense of who your team players are, what traits they have, what cues they encode. You notice certain human behaviors occurring as the group dynamic evolves.

As you continue to listen, and observe, and analyze the others carefully in your group, you gather the information that is infinitely more valuable to the team's success and the project's success than the feeble attempt as an informative presentation. Those details don't even seem important anymore. Because you have a team you can read, and it's easy to read that they already understand the problem more intimately than you will. Read them, trust your reading, and bring about the solution by proper management of the team, and not by trying to devise a solution yourself and then delegate its pieces.

Social Relations

In the same way that a sharp eye for emotional intelligence is required to be a leader, this same intelligence can contribute to an overall better structure for relationships, be it friendships in children or adults, intimate relationships, and other social engagements.

In children and teens, we see consistently that when a stronger EI is present, a better social interaction they will have. These children are a lot less frequently involved with acts of defiance or anti-social behavior. For adults, a similar result. A higher EI was indicative of relationships that did not involve aggression, anger, or superiority. However, those elements were more present in the relationships of individuals with lower EI. This same result, in various forms, is the same in adult relationships, whether they're platonic, familial, or romantic.

In the same studies, children, teens, and adults all demonstrated better negotiation skills when they also demonstrated a higher EI.

Academic and Professional Achievement

As you might imagine, these same EI skills that are helping to develop leaders and healthy relationships, are also generating a higher caliber of student and employee or entrepreneur. Interestingly, in the case of students, a higher EI indicates a greater overall understanding of and achievement with the knowledge, but not necessarily on the testing. IQ still proved to be a more important factor in testing.

In the professional arena, there are some interesting results as well. It seems that the workforce cannot be lumped together for the sake of this study. The result is a mixture of unclear information. What we do see is that it truly depends on what kind of job a person was being asked to do. A born leader, for example, generally has trouble working happily as repetitive labor, whether mental or physical. On the other hand, some individuals (often those with lower EI) were the happiest in the following roles and least happy in leadership roles.

Chapter 4: Reading Body Language

What does it mean to be able to read someone? What does it take to influence the way others read you? When reading, others are mentioned, at least in this book, what's really meant is a sizing up of several unspoken factors, either consciously or subconsciously.

A sizing-up usually consists of rapidly taking in details about someone's personal information and personality type based on body language, facial expression, appearance, and gesticulation. Surprisingly (or perhaps not so surprising), what you say with words only accounts for a small portion of someone's opinion about you. It was recently revealed in studies that body language, facial expression, and appearance all ranked higher in the forming of someone's opinion about another individual, so much so that these silent communications made up more than half of the basis for the opinion — speaking only accounted for about 15% of the basis for the opinion.

Whether we like it or not, appearance is most frequently the initial basis for an opinion to form. We're a very visual society, and we've come to know and trust the micro-information we gather within just seconds of seeing someone. Of course, that's not to say the first impression of someone is always entirely accurate. We're all aware of stories that illustrate the risks of judging someone based on their appearance. A beggar could be a prince under the outward appearance. The new employee could be the boss undercover. But this doesn't change the fact that we, as humans, process, visual information about someone the moment we see them. By and large, it's not even a conscious behavior; we're doing it unconsciously. A visual assessment like this has helped to keep us safe for thousands of years, so it's built into us.

But there is a difference between processing information to make educated guesses about someone, and consciously using that information to form a judgment of someone's value. This is where the real-life morals try to teach us about making impulsive judgments about someone; condemning them or idolizing them, based on their appearance. A dangerous practice indeed, and if this is your approach, it's only a matter of time before that backfires on you, too.

Though we may observe a person's hairstyle, clothing, shoes, or car in order to make relatively innocuous determinations about them, we do not need to weigh a person's value based upon these things. For example, a scruffy, unkempt look with dirty clothes and worn shoes may provide us with a rough estimation that this individual may not have the means to look good, or the individual may not put too much value on appearance him or herself. Both of these pieces of information can instantly help you to make a connection and build a rapport with someone, better than without. You may find as you connect, that there's an entirely different reason for the appearance, but it doesn't matter much, because you have not judged a person's value by these details. You've only used these details to form some sort of an idea about who someone is, and because you have virtually no value connected to any of it, it's easy for you to adapt your perception of someone as you go along.

Other unspoken cues continue to inform you and help to form a determination as you go along through the interaction. The way someone stands, whether they make eye contact, whether they use their hands and body to gesticulate or whether they remain calm and still. The movements of their eyebrows and their lips. All of these little details are being processed by us consciously or subconsciously and helping to create an idea of who someone is and what they're all about.

Reading the unspoken body language is a highly effective skill, but you can even read into someone's spoken communication for more unspoken clues. By paying attention to the tones and inflections someone uses, you can determine how they truly feel about a situation regardless of what they report to feel. It's often the words people don't say that reveal the most.

The best way to learn about reading others accurately, and broadcasting yourself deliberately, is to understand basic human behavior. By acquainting yourself more closely with our basic human instincts and tendencies, you'll be able to pick up twice as much information in an interactive as you used to. You'll begin to notice it in all the interactions you have, and you'll become more aware of when you do it, too. This alone will make you a much better persuasive communicator, but we can go further than that.

In this section, you'll gain clarity on which common basic concerns drive us as human beings, and how the persuasive individual can use this information to influence a situation by either reading it and responding to it, or by portraying it as a subtle, unspoken, manipulation. We'll focus for the most part on body language, gestures, and expressions, how to read them, and how to use them. By the end of this chapter, you should have enough information to start reading each interaction you find yourself in. Cognizant of your own broadcasting, and of theirs. You don't have to do anything with this information just yet necessarily. Training yourself to look and listen for it and recognize it is sufficient for now.

The Basics of Body Language

Think back to one of the most recent interactions you've had. Perhaps this was a situation at work, or at the store, or at a recent event. Take a moment to think back to that scene. Remember where you were, who was there, what was being discussed or done; think of the details of the moment. Try to see yourself there again. Now consider the posture you were standing with and the posture, others around you were holding. Ask yourself if anyone had their arms crossed. Were they looking toward the door?

Each of these small details is revealing information about you or about others around you. These details can be used to move the interaction along in a positive and beneficial way, or they can clue you into someone else's true intentions.

Posture is a common way for us to gauge someone's self-confidence and self-image. In a typical case, a slouching posture can be indicative of someone with a lower level of self-confidence and self-worth than someone who stands tall. However, a stance can be too aggressive or too close to the personal space of another, and you will be perceived as overbearing. Posture is one of the first pieces of body language we perceive to either consciously or subconsciously draw inferences from it about the person.

We pick up information about posture as soon as we get a visual of someone, but there is another tactic we can use discreetly to help you identify some basics about a prospect. The tactic is to look for certain clues that tell you whether your prospect is a visual, auditory, or kinesthetic sort of individual.

Though there are plenty of similarities amongst us in human behavior, one of the ways we differ from one another is by the ways in which our best digest information from the world around us. We use our five senses to register information, but one of our senses stands out as dominant against the others. This is typically indicative of the type of person you are and the ways in which you better digest details about your surroundings. There are three dominant senses we use to take in and retain information: visual, auditory, and kinesthetic. Though most of us use all of these senses for absorbing information

The Sight-Based Person

This personality type is the most common amongst us, making up about 75% of people. Concepts and memories are mainly stored in mind as visual images and pictures. When they speak, visual people tend to use language that pertains to vision in order to express themselves. For example, a visual person might say:

- "I'd like to get your **perspective**."
- "You're a **sight** for sore eyes."
- "That's not the **vision** I had in mind."

Physically, the visual person will generally stand with an upright, front-facing posture. This person is typically well-dressed and put together because they tend to be more concerned with their visual appearance.

When a visual individual is experiencing stress, it tends to be gathered and held in the shoulder area. This might look like the shoulders rounding and pulling up toward the ears, or it might look like the shoulders, pulling back and forcing the spinal area to stiffen. That's not to say all individuals with visible tension in their shoulders are absolutely visual people, but it's quite common, and it would be a smart piece of information to intuit, even if you end up changing your mind later based on more information about the person.

When visual people are trying to remember something, they tend to look upwards. This causes them to develop wrinkles in the center of the forehead. These individuals tend to have thin lips instead of full lips, which is subconsciously indicative of a responsible, practical, personality type. This individual is comfortable making regular eye contact, and they actually start to feel uneasy if others will not make eye contact with them. For this personality, eye contact is an important part of building trust in the rapport, and it's an indication to them that you're paying attention as they speak.

The Sound-Based Person

This personality type accounts for about 20% of the people we interact with. Concepts and memories are primarily stored in mind as sounds, noises, melodies, and quotes. When they speak, auditory people tend to use language that pertains to hearing and sound in order to express themselves. For example, an auditory person might say:

- "I want to **voice** my concerns."
- "Let's wait until we get the **word**."
- "A **bell** went off in my mind when I saw him."

Physically, the auditory personality type may not be as well-dressed or as concerned with appearance as the visual personality. This is because the visual representation of themselves to others is less important to them than the information; they share through talking, sound, and voice.

The auditory individual doesn't enjoy eye contact as much as visual people. In situations where eye contact would be normal, the auditory person may avoid it. Contrary to the way it may appear to some, this is not a sign of disrespect or disinterest. The auditory person looks down, looks at relevant papers, or moves a pen around on paper, making a subtle sound. This is actually the auditory person concentrating on what you're saying. Eye contact would be more uncomfortable and therefore, distracting. Rather than be distracted, the auditory individual is looking somewhere arbitrary in order to focus on the sound of what you're saying.

This is the type of personality that clicks their pen, taps their foot, or drums quietly on the table. This is the most effective way for these individuals to digest, process, and store information. They are creating a memorable and meaningful experience with the information to be saved in mind by sound patterns which makes the information easier to recall in the future.

The Touch-Based Person

This personality type is the hugger. They account for about 5% of the individuals we interact with. This is the type of individual who likes to get to know you by sharing personal space with you and touching in various ways. Like the visual and the auditory personalities, the kinesthetic person will speak in ways that use a touch- and feeling-based vocabulary. They might use phrases like:

- "I like to be **hands-on**."
- "Let's **put a pin** in it for now."
- "I have a bad **feeling** about this."

This individual wants to be near others and wants to get a sense of a person's "vibe" by spending time with them in the same (usually small) space. They tend to be the "touchy-feely" kind of person who prefers to build a rapport based on physicality and feelings. They love to connect with others, even in platonic ways, with a touch on the arm or shoulder. You'll always find the kinesthetic person dressed for comfort.

If you interact with kinesthetic people, or you are a kinesthetic personality yourself, it's important to keep a few things in mind for the most successful interactions. Remember that while kinesthetic people like to touch in order to communicate, not everyone else does. In fact, some people are very put off by physical contact. For some individuals, it's distracting to have their personal space disrupted, so they prefer not to hug or make affectionate gestures. It's important to respect both sides of the interaction and come to a sort of subconscious compromise.

If you're the kinesthetic person interacting with primarily visual and auditory people, acknowledge that the majority of people are not kinesthetic communicators; yours is a small category of individuals. While there are plenty of visual and auditory personalities that still appreciate hugs and the like, it's still not necessarily the way they best absorb information. When you're building a rapport, a touch can be a good thing, but if your intention is to educate or persuade an individual, you will want to use an approach that matches their personality type for the best results.

If you're a kinesthetic person testing the waters to see if others are receptive to touch, you can start slow and see how it goes, but you must pay attention and take notice of the subtle cues from the individual. An overbearing kinesthetic approach is the fastest to get shut down because instincts for protection subconsciously come up. Depending on the situation, it can be nice to start with a light and casual forms of contact, such as a handshake or an elbow-to-elbow bump as an accent to a conversation piece. As you build a rapport, you will be able to determine if you can communicate with this individual in a more tactical way.

If you're not the kinesthetic personality and you don't like to touch, you don't have to. But understand that most people do use the contact of some sort for basic communication so be prepared. If you're okay with a handshake, you can extend your hand a second before others, to subconsciously set a boundary of your personal space. If your hand is very extended from yourself, others will get the message to respect the space around your body. This establishes a point of contact for others but comfortably signals a boundary.

Gestures and Expressions

With a solid grasp on how we instinctively react, and which factors play a part in our reactions, you are capable of an overall assessment of someone (or yourself). Looking for clues of whether they are more likely to be visual, auditory, or kinesthetic will give you more insight and leverage for your interaction. But there's another layer deeper we can go. Next, let's take a look at the most commonly used subconscious expressions and gestures and what they mean.

Facial Expressions

An easy way to interpret someone's comfort level by looking at their faces is to pay attention to his or her eyebrows. Eyebrows can be very revealing about the level of relaxation for others around you. Eyebrows that relax to the outside of the brow are generally comfortable in the interaction. A raised eyebrow is often a sign of interest or skepticism. To determine which, try to look for other clues in gesture and expression. Both raised eyebrows are a sign that an individual is feeling surprised, fear, or worry.

The side glance is a subconscious movement that also reveals when an individual is nervous or uncomfortable. The eyes looking to the side are searching subconsciously for an exit from the interaction.

Lips can be a little more difficult to read, and the takeaway can be rather vague, but typically those with fuller, larger lips tend to be more free-spirited, childlike, and even immature. Those with thinner lips are perceived as more responsible and mature. Though we might not mean to, we do read into the shape of peoples' lips. Next time you're in a crowd, take note of whether individuals have thin or full lips and whether that trait seems to match up with other inferences you may be able to draw out from speech and body language.

Nodding is an interesting trait to observe because we (at least in the Western world) tend to use nods to mean a variety of things from mundane to sinister. The trick here, like eye contact, is in the context. A person could be nodding to signal you to hurry along with your conversation subconsciously. Or, they could be nodding because they want to express concern and care for your emotions, or agreement with your statements. Look for other behaviors that might help you to refine your assessment.

People tend to touch their jaw or chin with a hand when they're making decisions in their minds. However, there's a difference in doing this seriously, and doing this behavior to appear as though a decision is being made when one is really not. There is a long history of this gesture being linked to contemplation or decision-making. From Shakespeare to Bugs Bunny, people also make this gesture when they want you to think they are making a decision or consideration. For this reason, you should pay extra close attention to where the person's eyes are pointed when they do this. If a genuine decision is being made, the individual's eyes will likely be pointed down and to one side when they touch their jaw or chin. If this same gesture is made, but the person's eyes are looking straight ahead, or at you, the consideration is likely a false one.

Stance and feet are also an important communication tool to take note of. The distance between your feet, the direction they're pointing, and whether they're crossed can all be indications of how open a person is in conversation. If a person's feet are pointed toward you and a shoulder distance apart, they are likely more willing to share information with you and trust you. If the feet are pointing toward a door, close together, or crossed, the individual is guarded and may have some emotional walls up. If the feet are placed more than shoulder-distance apart, the stance is an aggressive one.

Crossed arms or legs are a strong subconscious sign that an individual is closed off to the interaction This may be out of an exaggerated need to protect oneself in general, but it could also be a sign that they are specifically untrusting of the person to whom they are conversing.

Now it's time to start paying attention. You're aware of human reactions that drive us, and you're aware of factors that play a role in how we react. It's time to start analyzing people for practice. When you're at a meeting, an event, or in line at the grocery store, examine the body language of those around you. Can you tell who communicates best with visual vocabulary and who the hugger is? Consider the body language you're giving off in these same places. Is it accurate? Is it the image you wish to be sent?

For the next seven days, make these observations about yourself and others in at least one scenario. In a notebook or on your phone, record the date and the interaction or place. Then record your observations. The goal is to become a keen observer and sharpen your people-reading skills over the seven days. At the end of seven days, look back over your observations, and see if they've become more observant and more accurate each day.

It's recommended that you continue this practice for a few weeks at least. This will help to program you to look for information on body language automatically, and it will help you to sharpen the image of yourself you want to broadcast. As you continue the assignment, remember to go back and analyze your entries to gauge how well you're progressing.

Chapter 5: From Analysis to Influence

In addition to what you already know, there are a few fundamental persuasion techniques to learn in order to capture your best results. Next, you'll review how to use metaphors and stories to strengthen and clarify your conversation, and how to use other persuasive conversation techniques like modeling, anchoring, and reframing. Coupling these techniques with the information you already know now about human reaction will deliver maximum benefit from your interaction.

Metaphors and Stories

As you already know, metaphors and stories are powerful tools for persuasion.
The best way to penetrate the rich soil of the subconscious imagination is with a story.

It's been suggested that there are only three or four types of stories that truly exist. The great comedy, the great tragedy, the great adventure, and the great metamorphosis are these basic premises. Every other story is just a copy of a different pen stroke. You can use these basic story forms to take the subconscious mind on an exciting and emotional roller coaster ride. In whichever form suits best, take the hero on his or her journey. Create a story to help the individual's subconscious mind experience the sensations of the desired outcome. The commercials use this method all the time. With subtle access to the subconscious mind through the use of metaphor, the mind will accept ideas and suggestions without resistance. Because the suggestions were made at a highly susceptible time, the individual will be profoundly affected by the words and can more easily move to the desired outcome without resistance. The stories are so relatable and potent for humans. You can use them to establish deliberate marks on the individual's subconscious.

Model and Emulate

There are several types of modeling that are used for persuasion, but one of the most commonly used versions is the act of modeling what the other person is doing in order to build a rapport subconsciously. When the person with whom you're speaking smiles, you to smile. Mimicking the person, you're talking with can quickly lower walls and help everyone to feel that you understand them and you're listening. You must temper this approach, however. Modeling everything, or at strange moments, can be suspicious and off-putting, making others feel almost as if you're offering sarcastic enthusiasm.

A very common example of modeling, we especially see today is modeling within chat, email, and SMS. In-text and chat, there's an initial common ground we generally all start at; polite, casual-professional, and though abbreviations may be a part of the text, slang is usually not. As we become more familiar with the people we talk to, we start to use slang. As one of us uses it, the other of us feel comfortable being more casual and also start to use slang. If one of us uses "lol," the other of us feel comfortable to start using abbreviated text slang. If one of us drops a swearword, the other of us feel less inhibited about watching what we say.

Similarly, if one of us gets a bit more casual in a text conversation, and the other of us does not follow suit, it can actually build a wall between the two. It could produce feelings of mistrust and perceived superiority.

Plant Expressions and Gestures

Anchoring is conditioning an individual for a certain response based on a sensory trigger like a handshake, an eyebrow movement, or the sound of a bell. It's well-known as a conditioning experiment, but Pavlov and his dogs are a good example of anchoring. The bell is the anchor, and sensory trigger used to make the dogs salivate.

Imagine sitting down at your job interview with the boss for the first time. Initial impressions are everything. You want to make sure the interviewer knows you are great in a leadership position. You know leadership is crucial to this role and the highest priority for the interviewer. Anchoring can work well for you here, discreetly and quickly. Pay attention to the interviewer's pace, tone, breathing, and body language as you listen.

When the interviewer takes time to talk to you about the importance of leadership in this role and the qualities of a leader, listen. When these qualities are mentioned, raise your eyebrow in a subtle way that still makes sense in the conversation, but disruptive enough subconsciously to make a mark on the interviewer's internal map of reality.

Each time these precious qualities are mentioned or described again, subtly and subconsciously anchor them to you with the movement of your eyebrows. A skilled persuader and reading body language may go the extra mile. Upon meeting the interviewer for the first time, the master would notice through body language that the interviewer is not comfortable making eye contact, in which case an eyebrow anchor would be lost. On the other hand, the skilled persuader can deduce that while the interviewer does not much care for eye contact, he or she is a very auditory person. The skilled persuader adapts at the last minute, substituting the eyebrow anchor for the clicking pen at the mention of these desired leadership qualities. Later, when the interviewer asks the skilled persuader to expand on leadership skills and experience, that visual or auditory trigger with the clicking pen can be used again to subconsciously link yourself to the desired traits in the mind of the interviewer.

If you ever saw Tony Robbins gives a motivational presentation, you may notice one of the physical anchors he has given himself and continues to use. He bumps the palms of his hands to his chest in an enthusiastic and competitive expression. This for Robbins is a physical trigger attached to intense feelings and sensory memories of mastery, power, and ecstasy. Each time he does this to himself, it's like giving himself a boost of that all-powerful nothing-can-stop-me-now feeling.

Reframe the Perspective

Another core technique is reframing. Similarly, to the other techniques, this is extremely versatile and effective, and it's great both for programming oneself and in persuading those around you in a positive way. Reframing is another naturally occurring process in our interaction and socialization. Unfortunately, we usually use it to hurt ourselves instead of help.

The idea of reframing is to take a situation that has been painted as negative by you or someone else and put a new spin on the situation that feels better and may not have been considered before.

For example, let's say there's a job interview you go to; you really want this job. The benefits are fantastic, and the salary is competitive and pays very well. After the job interview, you spend a great deal of time talking about that job opportunity and thinking about it. You start to plan out your budget based on this salary. About a week later, you find you didn't get the job, and you're upset. You talk to your friend who knows you wanted that job badly. You tell your friend you were so sure the job was yours. You tell your friend, someone there probably had it out for you and interfered. You blame other people, other circumstances, and you feel cheated.

Your friend helps you by taking this negative downward spiral of thoughts and reframes the situation for you. Your friend agrees that it's too bad you didn't get the job but suggests perhaps it's for the best. Your friend puts it in perspective and reminds you of the long hours, the commute, and the increased responsibility. Your friend suggests that even though you think you wanted that job, perhaps you didn't; it wasn't the right job for you. Your friend tells you the perfect job opportunity is still out there for you, but a step closer now. With this alternative view, you can put the situation into perspective, too. Things suddenly don't seem so final and negative. This friend has reframed the situation for you.

Reframing is also a powerful way to regain feelings of control in a moment that feels frustrating and overwhelming. Of course, you should reframe a negative emotion with a neutral or happy one. The replacement should feel good, not bad. If you don't feel perfect about your first attempts to reframe, don't give up. It takes practice.

Tactics of Influence for the Deliberate Communicator

There's another secret for you to learn if you want to be a productive influencer. This one practice, in particular, ensures you're the person in the room with the most control and the most confidence. This number one practice is so obvious that it's also the most overlooked. Most of us don't even think about the impact of this one practice because it's unconscious behavior. Breathe.

This not just a reminder to breathe. This is masterful advice to breathe strategically. Use a regulated breath. By taking deliberate control of your breath, especially in the tense moments, you can appear to be the cool and collected authority.

To practice strategic breathing, take your thumb and put it to your chest, just below where an underwire of a bra would be. Press into your flesh gently with your thumb and take a slow deep breath in. Notice whether you can feel your diaphragm pushing back on your thumb.

Next, put your hands around your chest as if you were going to pick yourself up. You'll notice your diaphragm stretches all the way around to your back. With your hands in place around your chest, take another deep and slow breath in and out again, and you'll be able to feel your diaphragm at work.

Stage actors and speakers have to perform diaphragm exercises with their voice coaches for a very good reason. The diaphragm holds a tremendous amount of power for you because it can be used to regulate your breath. When your breath is slow and steady, you appear to be in more control than those with erratic breathing. You look as though you're the least disrupted or upset, or worried. You appear to be the one who has it most together. This appearance, whether entirely true or not, is your key to being the most confident; the calmest and collected. Others will naturally look to you for guidance or help.

As a final note on strategic breathing, when it comes to regulating yourself and your reactions to stimuli: know when to close your mouth. When we speak, we pass our thoughts on our breath. We don't speak as we inhale; we speak as we exhale. Train your body to close your mouth when you inhale and open it to speak on the exhale. This is another sure sign of the well-regulated breath of a confident person.

For those who want to present themselves clearly and communicate persuasively, there's an important tactic that's almost as overlooked as deliberate breath. It's crucial to warm up your voice. Your voice is a primary instrument of persuasion.

A musician would never step out on stage without having tuned and warmed up on their instruments. An athlete would never perform a feat without a proper stretch first.

You will not be your most persuasive without warming up your voice first. Professional speakers, lawyers, politicians, and actors all use voice coaches to maximize the influence and persuasion they hold over their audience.

It's not just a suggestion; it's a serious technique to maximize the results of an individual's output. Give yourself time to warm up your voice before you speak.

There are many ways to do this, and there are several very popular practices for warming up, but one of the most popular is to sing. Sing to yourself in the shower in the morning, or in the car on the way to work. Talk to yourself in the mirror. Record yourself talking on your cell phone and listen back.

If you speak often, or you're planning to, consider developing a warm-up routine that you can do in less than a minute to yourself before you begin speaking. Practice changing your pitch, tone, volume, speed, and silence. Experiment with your timbre and register, notes, prosody, and pacing. These can all be used to draw emphasis, create an emotion or response, and to bypass the critical mind for direct access to the impressionable subconscious mind. Use them all to paint your voice as an artist would use paints and brushes to design a masterpiece.

There is an infinite number of phrases and combinations of words that can be extremely persuasive in the right scenarios, but there are four key phrases that can be utilized in most everyday interactions to influence those around you. These four phrases, or versions similar, are used by some of the world's most persuasive speakers and sales professionals. They're versatile, fast, and effective in almost any situation. When you have the opportunity, try using one or more of these phrases to influence a conversation or decision.

In some interactions, passive-aggressive communication can be a huge influence.

This is one of those communication methods. You propose to your audience (subtly and discreetly) that either they comply with the path that leads to the outcome you want, or they will be faced with the same problems they face today. Take, for example, a salesperson trying to close a deal on a home. The salesperson might implement a sentence like, "Either we do what we need to do to get you into this house by the end of the month, or you're going to keep on living in a neighborhood you don't like, with a school you don't like, in a home that's too small."

Asking for help can be an excellent persuasive tactic, even if you don't actually need help. When you ask someone for their help, it's an implication that you're confident they can help, but also that you can trust them. This is an ego boost, which can go a long way in an interaction. With a phrase like this, you can get someone to help you or execute a task for you.

When you ask for help from others around you, it also puts those individuals in a social situation which requires them to make a decision about whether to help you or not. The decision is often needed on the spot and out loud. People don't want to create uncomfortable confrontation by saying they won't help, so they will usually comply. In some cases, individuals might be concerned that they will be seen as rude or uncaring if they do not comply with helping.

Asking for help can also be used as a setup to a larger favor you intend to ask in the future. For example, you might ask your new acquaintance if you can borrow a dollar for a snack. You eventually give the dollar back as you should. But it's really a setup scenario. You gave the dollar back to gain your acquaintance's trust and show yourself in a trustworthy individual, because you intend to ask for a bigger favor in the future, such as a larger amount of money.

"Imagine" is a magic word that ignites the impressionable subconscious mind. Access to this part of the mind can obviously be used to generate influence and sway opinions. This word can be used in many situations to draw out the creative mind and get it to follow you to the outcome you desire. When using the word, it's often paired with the sensory perceptions that are important for the subconscious mind to become greatly enthralled with your story. This could be done by reminding your prospect of smells, prompting them to imagine a location or the sound of birds, or any kind of tactile experience such as warm towels right out of the dryer. The more sensory perception you refer to in the minds of your imagining audience, the stronger the story will be in their subconscious minds. When you're practicing persuasion on yourself or others, activate the subconscious with this word and enhance it by utilizing metaphor and story with it. Attempt to persuade your audience by guiding them to imagine the benefits of a certain goal or outcome.

Two little letters can do so much. "If" is another powerful word that can be used similarly to the way you might use the word "imagine." "If," asks your audience to break from critical, logical thought, suspend their beliefs, and engage the imagination in another possibility; one where the desired outcome is achieved.

By presenting to your audience an if/then scenario, the imagination is automatically engaged in order to understand the concept you are trying to communicate fully. They basically have to listen and conjure the scenario in the imagination to digest the information you're sharing.

Positive Persuasion

It's not so much about crossing a line; it's about your true intentions. The difference between negative and positive manipulation is not necessarily whether it's covert, or whether it attempts to change a belief; it's about ethics.

If you can be relatively sure you're going against a core belief or something your prospect would not want, it's not ethical.

If you would not want it done to you, it's probably not ethical.

If it causes harm to your prospect, it's probably not ethical.

If you have to threaten or force someone to do something, it's coercion, and it's definitely unethical.

You can use the art of persuasion and manipulation without being two-faced and deceptive. There's nothing wrong with wanting it all. You deserve what you want, and you can have it, but you must remember that if you're entitled to what you want, so is everyone around you. You must use your powers for good and not diminish anyone else's pursuit of happiness. Respect the others around you, and respect the art. You'll experience a greater sense of accomplishment and pride.

Knowledge of these basic concepts isn't hard, but people are largely unaware of them, or aware of them on a subconscious level only. Learning the art of influence and how to apply these techniques puts you ahead of the crowd. With this information, you have a tool kit to use in any interaction you have. You'll be able to manage the interaction with confidence and authority and communicate your intentions and expectations clearly. Then all you have left is to watch the situation play out as you desire.

It may be true that there are individuals, businesses, politicians, and leaders out there who conduct underhanded, dirty, mean business. They use knowledge and tools in harmful ways. But that doesn't mean all businesses run that way, and it doesn't mean you have to conduct yourself like that.

Hidden in the folds of your life experiences are powerful lessons about why manipulation and persuasion can be a wonderful thing. Imagine for a moment, the cardboard boxes the Chinese takeout comes in. These cardboard boxes are usually made of a folded waxy paper. These boxes are convenient for packing, easy to open, easy to set out, and easy to share. These boxes are also very eco-friendly. Being that they're made of cardboard, they can be rinsed and recycled. For the lazy diner, these boxes save you the work plating because they work perfectly as serving bowls, too, so fewer dishes are used and less cleanup is necessary. But these boxes are even more practical and more useful than that; more than most people realize.

As you've sat and enjoyed your Chinese takeout delights, chances are you've never even noticed that the folds of those boxes open up. When you open the folds of a Chinese takeout box, the box actually becomes a convenient plate or bowl for the diner. The box opens out to hold the contents in a convenient, shallow, serving bowl, or plate for yourself. It fits comfortably in the palm of one hand so the diner can use the other hand to manage utensils. If you just give a little tug to the edges of that box, it will open, and you can fit two or three times the amount of food. And still, you'll probably never see others open the paper box. No one questioned it.

No one manipulated the edges to get more out of it. If you're sitting at the table serving dishes and plates you'll have to clean, don't feel bad. This is all changing for you with your new embrace of positive manipulation. The box probably goes its short lifetime without ever stretching to its full potential. How many other little paper boxes are you missing out on in your life?

Without a bit of questioning and a bit of manipulation of the objects in your environment, the potential would be lost. Do not squander this skill, but rather, nurture it and learn to use it to benefit yourself and those you love. Be brave enough and thoughtful enough to tug and poke at the folds. Look for the bits you can pull on to get the full potential of what you want.

Manipulation can help to strengthen communities. For example, manipulation can be used to raise awareness for an important topic, or it can be used to raise funds for a beneficial goal. Positive social manipulation can help save entire communities. In the case of public transport, it could save entire cities and nations.

In 2001, the 911 attack on the Twin Towers in New York City prompted the institution of the Transportation Security Administration (the TSA) at airports and other high-traffic public transportation. At first, it took a while for individuals to be comfortable with the extra time and responsibility it now required to ride planes and public transport, but it didn't take long for most to accept this as a fair compromise for a safer ride. Now, this is just a standard part of travel that everyone plans for. It has been in the many campaigns just after the attack, which demanded increased security, which ultimately led to this implementation. This new security protects millions of us every day, thanks to the social manipulation of new laws being put in place.

More recently, another positive social manipulation has taken place with respect to the attack in 2001. Political activist, journalist, and actor Jon Stewart have successfully seen his 9/11 Fund Bill passed in Congress. Stewart's relentless positive social manipulation has made a significant impact on the 9/11 responders. A fund had been set up to help first responders and victims of the attack, but recently Stewart noted the fund was almost empty. His consistent and confident attempts to persuade Congress to make it a priority to fill the fund again has made it so. This is of incredible import, as many of these first responders are only now able to begin rebuilding their lives. In addition, these heroes have only now started to learn about illnesses caused by their service in the attack. It's imperative that our nation supports these individuals and make sure a continued fund is available for some time to come.

Persuasion can work for the betterment of one party, both parties, or for the betterment of a mass group, society. We see persuasion at work in trial courts as lawyers persuade the jury of someone's innocence or guilt. We see persuasion at work, in politics as leaders persuade us to vote in one direction or another. We see persuasion at work in every single entertainment blockbuster as the actors persuade us to believe this story is real and machines have taken over. We all use persuasion every day, whether we are doing it with an artful skill or sloppily and without focus. Persuasion is not automatically corrupt; it's just leading others to believe something that suits us. And maybe them. This is just one of the many tactics we use to communicate.

Chapter 6: Seduction, Manipulation, and Lying

By now, you have a clear understanding of what the art of manipulation is, and you know of several historical examples of it. You've seen it at work in today's media, and you can find examples of this art in the works of coaches, trainers, lawyers, politicians, and other leaders.

But you also know there's more to influence a situation than that. A skilled influencer must be aware of basic human and social behavior. This artist should be aware of whether others are visual, auditory, or kinesthetic; the artist should be aware of which he or she is.

Influencing Others

If you've done something to influence a situation or an individual, it means you've demonstrated the ability to directly, or indirectly, affect the development of a situation, to affect an outcome, or to affect the behavior or action of an individual or group of individuals. Having influence over something or someone is typically a practice of persuasion, but without necessitating any need for change in the individual's belief paradigm. Influencers often recognize the beliefs that an individual or group already holds, but the beliefs are either irrelevant for the situation, or can be utilized to help the influencer makes a stronger point. What the influencer typically does not do, is attempting to change a core belief. Changing core beliefs in others is sometimes the goal, but this is more easily understood as an active attempt at manipulation.

If you were to think of the art of influence as a process, you'd begin as an influencer; an apprentice of the art. As you gain an understanding of how to be an effective influence, you graduate to the next level: persuasion. This is an advanced level of influence; a more deliberate practice. As you sharpen the skill set of persuasion, you naturally flow into the next level of the art: seduction. This is a master of influence; well-practiced with many failed attempts as well as successes. At this point, you'd know exactly how to entice almost anyone, in almost any interaction you can imagine and confident in doing so. This might be a romantic seduction, or it could be a sale, seduction, but in either case, your power of persuasion is strong, and as such, your prospects are easily enticed.

Up until this point, your practice has been mostly transparent, with no significant attempt to change or go against an individual's core beliefs. But if you're going for your black belt in the art of influence, you have one more step to master: the art of manipulation. Manipulation is often an effect on someone or something in a more-or-less covert fashion, rather than a transparent operation. Manipulation may also involve an attempt to change a core belief, or set of beliefs for an individual or a group.

Though these skills are starting to sound more nefarious, keep in mind it doesn't have to be this way. As we will see, there are many examples of a covert attempt to manipulate core beliefs which are all still positive examples. A perfect example of this is cognitive-behavioral therapy. While much of this type of therapy is transparent and very interactive for both the patient and the therapist, there are still aspects of this practice that are done on a covert, discreet, level of the therapist. This is done purely to maximize the benefits of therapy for the patient. A patient may hold a very self-deprecating thought; repeating this thought in various ways, and experiencing examples of it throughout each day.

A belief is just a thought that has been repeated enough times. The more times a thought is repeated, the more solid it becomes as the experience and the reality. A therapist will covertly uncover the negative thought patterns and attempt to manipulate the pattern. More specifically, the therapist intends to interrupt the negative thought-pattern and replace it with a positive self-serving thought. The positive thought, repeated enough times, becomes the belief. This is, of course, an oversimplification of the entire therapeutic process, but it serves as a positive example of manipulation.

If you've made it to the point of practicing positive manipulation, you are a master of the art of influence. But what happens when you take the positive aspect away? What does it look like when a manipulation goes from positive to negative?

Seduction is Like Selling

You've come quite far in your desire to learn how to lead a more influential and persuasive lifestyle. There are dozens of methods you're now aware of for use in analyzing someone in just about any social interaction you can imagine.

You've developed a solid foundation of practices you can take up today, to improve the level of confidence, authority, and calm coming from your body and your voice. You know how to spot subconscious information and how to deliver it.

If you've been practicing these concepts and techniques in your daily life as you've been reading this book, then you've been developing and sharpening your own abilities as you've learned. There's a good chance that you're already an effective influence. Perhaps you've even begun to practice deliberate and discreet persuasion and manipulation to see if you can bring about a certain result. In this section, you'll learn how to apply a few more tools to maximize your results. It's a bit like you've evolved from a stock car to a slick race car and you're about to get some nitrous tanks.

Persuasion through seduction and selling is very similar. In fact, the lines often blur between the two. There's no better place to look for a plethora of examples, than inside the entertainment industry. By and large, the entertainment industry *is* seduction for sale. Not only is sex used widely in movies, music, vlogs, and in social media, but that's really only the tip of the sexy iceberg. The seduction used in the media has such a broad and powerful reach that it ends up seducing us in other industries as well, like fashion, for example.

We generally all want to be seductive and attractive to others, or we want others to seduce us. Often both. The manipulative tentacles of the entertainment industry wrap around these desires and tell us how to have them. Use this makeup, wear these clothes, drive this car, change your shape, listen to this music. Our inherent drives take over because we want to seduce or be seduced. These industries surely how down the ways in which they can influence and manipulate the public.

Ultimately, all marketing is about seduction and that generally requires a strong understanding of human behavior, especially when it comes to communication and social situations. Whether you're marketing yourself for social networking, a business situation, or a romantic one, knowing how to read and apply information about human behavior is critical to your success.

When you boil it down, there's not a lot of difference between seduction and selling. When we're talking about either, we're talking about the action of persuading someone to believe or want something. Whether we're selling or dating, we do this by tempting and attracting our prospects. In either case, we're enticing prospects to join us in something rather risky and exciting; even something thought to be foolish or dangerous.

The obvious difference is determining the appropriateness of each situation. Though the two situations are nearly identical in many ways, there are some things you would do for a business situation, that would not be appropriate romantically. Likewise, there are actions you might take in a romantic encounter that would certainly be inappropriate in a business situation. However, it's incredibly common for these to overlap as well. There are plenty of examples of sex used as part of a business seduction. Knowing where the line is drawn is up to you. Because the two are so similar, we'll look at them in the same way as we move through these examples. It will be necessary for you to shape and mold to a given situation as you go. Use what you already know about what drives human response to determine the appropriateness of the situation. With a bit of tailoring, you can use any of these practices in a romantic capacity or a business one.

How do you tailor these tools for the situation? This is a combination of common sense and attention to reading your prospect. If you pay attention to your prospect, they will tell you with their body language and voice what it is you need to do to entice them. Pay attention to the formality of your language and presentation. It's comparable to whether you should wear casual clothes or formal ones. Also, pay attention to the speed that your train is traveling. In both business and sex, moving too fast with someone will put them on their guard. Watch for how receptive your prospect is. The following set of skills and techniques can be used to gain new customers, close deals, or seduce romantic partners.

With this information, you'll be more aware of signs of attempted manipulation on you, and you'll know exactly how to manage that interaction when you see it. Manipulating a manipulator is a champion test for you, as you continue to learn and apply influential tactics in your everyday life.

More tests, assignments, and practice are all in your future. It will serve you well to begin and continue the exercises toward the end of this section. Completing this book should only be the beginning for you, in the journey to becoming an expert influencer; a professional persuader; a master manipulator. Take the extra time to read through the exercises at the end and select a few you're willing to practice regularly.

Avoid Manipulation and Deception

Leading others to believe in or support something doesn't necessarily mean the persuasion is negative. We use persuasion in many different ways every day to navigate the world and cope with ever-changing circumstances. A wife may persuade her husband that the vacation they really want this year is Bali; not another trip to Miami. A child on the playground may persuade a friend to trade one Pokémon card for another. The teacher persuades the class to sit down. The veterinarian persuades the puppy to sit still. The store clerk persuades you to get one more; it's cheaper in bulk. The CDC persuades everyone to stay inside and seal the windows.

These manipulations are not necessarily trying to take advantage of someone. In all of these cases, it can be argued that the influence is even intended to benefit the other person (or dog) at least a bit. Maybe a lot.

But where do we draw the line? When does manipulation stop coming from a positive intention and start to become deceptive and forceful? Is it my fault for persuading you, or your fault for being persuaded?

You may be deceptive and secretive to those around you, but ultimately, you cannot lie to yourself. You know if you're using persuasion in a corrupt way or not. You should strive to do no harm; you should strive to manipulate in a way that doesn't involve making people do things they don't want to do, or that would be harmful to them.

If you intend to be skillful at reading others and persuading them, you should be aware of the variety of conversational arenas in which you'll find yourself by deliberate or circumstantial means. It's valuable to gain familiarity with all of these types of persuasive communication, whether for your own use or your own protection.

Reverse Psychology

This tactic of persuasion is another we hear so often in the media and movies. We are overburdened with examples of this all around us. We see entertainment full of relatable examples of parents implementing reverse psychology to get their children to act a certain way or complete a task. An example of this might be the father of two siblings on the birthday of the younger sibling. The older sibling has not yet given a present to the birthday sibling. The father might suggest this is the case because the older sibling is selfish, stingy, and greedy and doesn't really love the younger sibling. Thus, the older sibling buys and presents a gift to the younger sibling. This is the result the father wanted all along.

Why did this work? People like to believe they are in control of themselves and their situations. When the father, or someone, proposes the challenge that they are not truly in control of themselves, the person immediately wants to change this, regardless of whether the action originally goes against their desires or not.

Deception

To deceive someone is not necessarily to lie. It's easy enough to deceive someone without stating any untruth. Deception is a cunning way in which information is presented, the truth or not, in a way that persuades the listener to think and feel a certain way about that information and the inferences that can be made of that information.

You can deceive without lying, but you cannot lie without deceiving. The trick in a successful deception is to trot out information that will support your case (whether or not it's factual) and apply language artfully in an attempt to make someone feel a particular emotion or agree with a particular line of thinking. Liars can often justify their actions in this way. It's important to pay attention to the words that are spoken and how they are spoken in order to get the truth.

A great example of this is something we see every day. When you visit the grocery store to buy some beef for burgers, you see a sticker with a claim: All natural, organic beef. The sticker doesn't trot out all the information; it's deceptive. It does tell you the beef is all-natural organic. It doesn't tell you that it is, typically, but not always the case. That beef might be made with three organically fed cattle and one old toxic-ridden cow. The sticker doesn't offer all the facts and information, just the ones that will best serve the image they try to maintain. Deceptive.

Mind Games

Arguably, mind games begin to cross into the nefarious dark because they are almost always used for the intent and benefit of the manipulator and teeter on whether these games coerce the subject in some way.

We very often see mind games played in romantic relationships and family relationships. This could be due to the wealth of resource knowledge you may have known someone for a long time, as opposed to just meeting them today. That's not to say you cannot play mind games with folks you just meet. This is sometimes used by street performers and magicians. But it's much more common to hear about and experience mind games within established relationships.

When someone uses mind games such as projecting, guilt-tripping, withholding affection, and gaslighting, on another individual, it's hard to defend these tactics as positive persuasion. Projecting, for example, is not a heinous crime, but it's certainly not a help to anyone but yourself to assume another individual feels the way you feel. This is typically a sign of self-centeredness and disregard for the feelings of others. When you begin to use this behavior to get what you want, it falls on the blurry line of manipulating others to do what they do not want to do. Very similarly, guilt-tripping, withholding affection, and gaslighting are not the very worst psychological tactics one could use, but they are definitely on that blurry line. Can these tactics be used in a more positive way? Absolutely. It's possible that an individual may employ these tactics to mitigate the psychological abuse being dealt with them by another. These tactics could become coping mechanisms under the right circumstance. It's important to keep in mind that by and large, these kinds of behaviors may seem tempting to get what you want, but if you examine the entire situation and the consequences of these tactics, you may find using them is not in alignment with what you really want at all.

Brainwashing

We move even closer to the dark side of psychology when we discuss brainwashing and mind control. This tactic is difficult to defend. The vast majority of examples of brainwashing and mind control are coercion. It seems obvious to say if the individual really wanted the outcome, the brainwashing would not be unnecessary. By definition, brainwashing applies systematic and forcible means to persuade someone into a new set of beliefs. It's the systematic and forcible approach to persuasion that truly puts this technique on the dark side. A compulsory indoctrination (social, political, religious, or otherwise) beliefs are coercive. When we hear brainwashing, we think perhaps of Prisoners of War and cult followers who may be subjected to this tactic and those like in order to break down the will and identity of the individual.

Beyond these dramatic cases of brainwashing, a shady but less nefarious version confronts us: subliminal messages. Not only does the media report on these stories, but marketing employs these tactics constantly. Remember the song that praises Satan when you listen to it backward or upside down? The media hypes examples of subliminal messaging like this (by preying on our fear of being subliminally controlled).

A much less vicious example is the recent change of Wendy's fast-food logo. The new icon cleverly uses a bit of subliminal messaging right below the friendly face of Wendy. Wendy's shirt collar is drawn in such a way that it depicts the scrolled word "Mom." This evokes a sense of home-cooked goodness when we see it. As you might have figured out, too, it utilizes anchoring to link that home-cooked goodness to the logo and to the excitement and satisfaction we feel when ordering and opening our Wendy's bag of food.

Triggering the Fear Response in Media

In the media today, we often see examples of people being manipulated to feel, think, and act a certain way through the use of fear. Whether the threat is significant or minuscule, whether the likelihood is high or low, people react to fear. It's an inherent response left from the days when survival was a daily struggle.

It continues to help us now, to prepare for, or defend against, any kind of negative impact on our circumstance. We use this inherent behavior to mitigate damage in our lives. Marketing and media recognize this inherent, widely-shared, similar behavior, and use it to gain our attention and influence us to think and respond in a particular way.

A common yet relatively benign example of media using fear as an influence on a large number of people can be found in news-weather reporting. Often times, storms and severe weather are teased to an audience. The audience sees this and becomes concerned; "how will this weather affect me and my plans?"

The audience tunes into the report to find out, so there's already one level of the manipulation taking place; the one that makes us tune into their broadcast. Next, the weather report might dramatize the incoming weather and play up worst-case scenarios. It's not uncommon for weather reports to suggest to the audience that they stock up for incoming severe storms.

As a result, local stores are sold out of bottled water, food, and other supplies. In some cases, the storm that arrives is much less eventful than originally hyped, and the stock up was not really necessary. Yet by playing on fear, and our basic need to protect ourselves from harm or discomfort, the media was able to affect an entire region's economy.

A somewhat more drastic example of using fear in the media is found in the 1980s in the UK, but this instance spanned decades and affected the global economy. It's probably unlikely that you've heard of, or can even easily pronounce bovine spongiform encephalopathy. It's much more commonly known as mad cow disease, which you likely have heard of, even if you're not entirely sure what it is.

Initially, bovine spongiform encephalopathy was discovered in the UK as a neurodegenerative disease amongst the cows. Though it was possible for the disease to be passed to humans, it was highly unlikely. But headlines about a disease that only affects cows weren't selling.

A clever newspaper marketer realized that if he played upon natural human fears, then he could sell more headlines and more papers. Instead of printing a headline and article about the risks that cows face by contracting bovine spongiform encephalopathy, he focused on what it could do to humans. He stopped calling it bovine spongiform encephalopathy and created a shorter and more sensational name for readers to call it: mad cow disease.

Readers immediately started reacting to the name as if it was reminiscent of rabies. The reporter again used natural fear to influence the public by linking risks to something many people were doing: eating beef. In rare cases, mad cow disease could be transmitted to humans by eating contaminated beef. The probability of this happening was quite low but highly sensational.

With a few deliberate changes to the way he was communicating, the reporter manipulated the public with fears of mad cow disease and as a result, affected the global beef economy from the 1980s until about 2005.

How to Lie

Smiles can be very revealing, but not to expose a candidate for a great friend or trustworthy partner. Rather, to find out who is a liar. When a person exhibits a normal, healthy, happy smile, the eyes are involved in that expression. The individual's lips will smile, but the eyes will, too. Smiling eyes have small crinkles at the outer corners of the eyes. Smiling eyes are a very difficult technique and muscle movement to fake deliberately. Attempt to fake them on your own face in a mirror. You'll be able to tell something looks "off"; wrong. This is what your audience sees when they receive a fake smile from you. They can tell something's off, at least on a subconscious level, and you'll start to generate feelings of skepticism and distrust among your audience.

If there is one last fundamental technique a beginner of positive persuasion and manipulation should learn, it's how to be a good liar. Most likely, you've told at least one lie in your lifetime, but are you good at lying or does your lack of persuasive skills reveal you as a liar? Lying, while generally looked down upon, is actually another unavoidable mechanism for communication. Whether you've been the spider or the fly, in a big web or a modest one, you know that lying is a part of life. Sometimes a little white lie helps if you've missed an appointment, or if you're trying to hurry someone else along. Sometimes the most well-intentioned lies backfire. Save yourself from backfiring by learning and practicing these skills for constructive lying.

Try paltering first. This is referred to commonly, especially by politicians, as the ethical lie. The ethical lie is a practice in the deception without technically lying. An example of this might be when a father asks his teenage daughter if she has been out with a boy all night. The daughter replies, "I went to Jane's house to do homework!" This is technically not a lie. If the father calls Jane's house, Jane's mother will verify that his daughter was there with Jane doing homework. What the deception does not clearly explain, is that after the homework at Jane's, the daughter did meet up with a boy to hang out for the rest of the night.

Believe your own lies if possible. This will help you to enjoy the process of sharing them. Bad liars try to get the lie over with as quickly as they can, and this almost always leads to a messy lie that backfires. Base your lie in some truth so that it's easier for you to justify to yourself and believe. This can also help you to remember your lie. If you're lying to someone you know, like a boss, keeping your lie based on some truth that your boss is aware of. This way, it will be more easily accepted.

Keep your story simple. Sometimes people think that by including all kinds of extra details, the story is made more believable. This, however, tends to have the opposite effect. Typically, a truthful story does not include all the extra details. A truthful story generally only includes the details that are relevant and important to the audience. When you start to include random details, the audience becomes suspicious of it. When a child tells a lie, this is often a revealing mistake that catches them in a lie. As adults, we remember that and feel skeptical when it happens to us as the audience.

Don't be overly dramatic. Subtly is your friend. If you lie out with exaggerated gesticulation or drama, it doesn't sound like the truth. It sounds like you're working extra hard to cover up a lie. Imagine a colleague trying to get out of work early. When the manager walks through the office to see how the day is going, the colleague fakes a dramatic cough and wheeze and mumbles something about not feeling well. If your colleague isn't careful, this is going to be a sign of an obvious deception.

Keep your lies in check. Knowing how to lie effectively doesn't mean you should tell lies without regard. Being a good liar means being a responsible liar. If you can tell the truth, you should. It's easier for you, and it's easier for others to believe you when you do actually use a lie tactic. Liars are often caught because they tell so many lies to so many people that their stories are no longer consistent. Lying well should mean lying less for a well-practiced persuasive communicator.

Improve Relationships with Analysis

Since you've developed a keen attention to reading those around you, and since you've become a bit of a professional persuader, you can use your new skills to repair existing relationships that may be experiencing some stress or tension. If you intend to use these skills to repair damaged ties, take extra caution to use them wisely. If you think you can simply coerce others into repair, you're wrong. Studies had recently shown that when the negative manipulation and coercion were used in romantic arguments, it drove partners away from each other with greater speed and intensity than other tactics used.

It should be your best and the most genuine intention to bring about a resolution that feels good and benefits both of you. Influence and persuasion can be used responsibly to repair a damaged relationship if used with deliberate positive intentions. Watch yourself when it comes to manipulation. While manipulation, too, can be positive under the right circumstances, it's not necessarily the right set of tools for repairing a relationship.

It would be best if you're able to be face to face with the individual you want to mend ties with. This gives you the best possible opportunity to pick up on all the conscious and subconscious communication being shared with you. It also gives you the very best opportunity to broadcast and emphasize deliberately with your own face, body, and voice. If you can find a quiet spot, conducive for the both of you, in public or private, it will be more likely that each of you will approach the interaction with more relaxation and less defensiveness. Being physically in a place where you both feel safe and comfortable will play a large part in the repair even before you begin.

Be cognizant of how precious your relationship is. There's a good chance the history of your relationship is rich and deep. Both of you have contributed to the relationship in your respective ways, and you should both be given credit for how much has been done and shared. It should be noted that many relationships in life never go so deep or have so much significance, and this is a large drive for your wanting to repair the relationship. Be respectful of the other person.

Use some of the different techniques you now know to prompt and inspire feelings of love and appreciation:

Use touch: If it's appropriate, touch the other person in a way that allows you to express compassion and care toward them. This could be a touch on the back of the shoulder, or it might be a hug or embrace. Don't force a touch if it's not the right timing or the most appropriate context, as doing so will likely backfire and give the other person doubt as to whether repairing this relationship is really the best decision.

Read the other person: Determine if the other person is more receptive to visual, auditory, or kinesthetic conversation and act accordingly. If possible, try to meet in a location that's conducive to their personality type. Meeting at a spot in nature for a walk or a picnic might be a perfect place for the visual person to feel comfortable. The auditory person might feel better meeting in a public park or a cafe where the background sounds of the city are an auditory comfort. The kinesthetic person might enjoy sharing an activity such as basketball, a hike, or a day at the beach where there tend to be many enticing tactile experiences.

Use body language: Direct your shoulders and feet toward the other person. Keep your arms and legs uncrossed. If it's acceptable, hold eye contact with the other person to show that you're listening carefully and understanding them. Model their gestures, expressions, and behaviors when you notice that they subconsciously make them. Regulate your breathing deliberately to maintain a calm and clear-headed disposition.

Use reframing: Help the other person to see past events or future worries in a different light. Putting scenarios from a different perspective reminds the other person that you're trying to be logical and fair.

Use your superpowers: Listen to the other person actively. Smile when they smile at you to return their attempt to bridge the gap and show caring. Show that you're vulnerable and recognize when they put themselves on the line with vulnerability, too. Be empathetic to the other person's position and perspective. Put yourself in their shoes and try to imagine how the other person feels instead of focusing purely on your own feelings. Show understanding and forgiveness. If you're willing to extend this level of acceptance to the other person, there's a much greater chance they will show you the same understanding.

Using these techniques in conjunction with keen attention to the other person's physical and vocal communications will make it easy for you to speak with this individual and mend ways amicably.

Chapter 7: Practical Application

In such a short time, you've become familiar with which techniques to use and when. You understand why and how to capture the attention of another and how to read what they are encoding.

Now you know that once you have that attention, you know how to hold it, how to deepen it, and how to access the imagination in order to plant powerful and influential ideas with both verbal and nonverbal communication. You know which types of body language will tell you to stay away from someone or when to move closer. You can imagine how to apply these techniques responsibly in your professional life as well as your personal life.

How does it feel to have a solid understanding of how to improve your communication style right now for better results? How does it feel to know with continued practice, you can master any social interaction and get what you want?

You have mastered this class. Now, implement it in your life. The more you practice the techniques and principles you've learned, the easier it becomes to do it. Soon, reading the silent broadcasts of others will be as easy as reading a name tag.

Are there areas of your circumstance you'd like to improve? Pay attention to your own broadcasting and how you can alter it. Whether it's your posture or your eye contact, you have the information you need to make a deliberate broadcast. Practice how you'd like your broadcast to go to yourself in the mirror or on camera.

The more you practice, the better you are at these skills. Select a couple of persuasive techniques you'd like to try. Think of a good place to test them out and put yourself there to test them. Don't stop at just testing them out. This isn't an offhand application. The art of analyzing others and using emotional intelligence is a highly structured and formulaic application of communication.

What You Can Do for Better Results

Follow these tips and tricks below, and with regular practice, you can be the most composed, and most compelling individual in the room.

Keep a hand-written or even cloud-based journal of your results each time you set out to test. Consider what you want the outcome to be, and how close you get to that goal. It will be equally as beneficial to record details like your environment, mood, mood, and the broadcast of the people in your environment, other influences, unplanned events, and so forth. While this sounds like a bit of effort, it pays off. The patterns that become visible to you is useful information that can be used for your end goal.

Some of these exercises will resonate with you more strongly than others. Stick to the ones you like and don't force yourself to engage in exercises that feel uncomfortable or stressed, as these may only increase feelings of self-doubt or wrong-doing.

Some exercises may sound too simple or silly for you, but you're encouraged to give each exercise and technique a chance. It's not unusual to find that the simplest concepts are actually the trickiest; the silliest seeming practices may be the most revealing.

Humans are creatures of habit. Rather than try to break that, your aim is to use it. Set a time to meditate each day. Make it approximately the same time each day, too, so that that body physiologically learns the new and healthy patterns you're implementing.

Take time at the moment. Some of these exercises will require you to be in the midst of an unhealthy or negative idea forming before you can use the techniques. In addition to setting aside specific times to practice, include spontaneous practice. Use a few exercises or techniques that require no preparation, special location, or specific materials for your spontaneous practice.

Be patient with yourself. You've been trained very well to overanalyze and self-criticize, so it will take a little practice before you start to dissolve those patterns and establish new ones. Being patient, gentle, and forgiving with yourself in this process will teach you to be the same way with yourself in future endeavors.

Be patient with others. Others may not be as ready and as open as you to understanding this and making positive changes. That's okay. It's not your job to make them ready, and it's not your job to teach them. Your focus is on your behaviors and your practice and improvement of deliberate communication. If others are interested in the changes you're making, it may feel comfortable and nice to share this information with them and listen to the information they have about these ideas. When others aren't interested or are made uncomfortable, don't force it.

Don't stop here. This is only the beginning. This information has primed you to go into the world and discover the world of positive and deliberate influence.

Exercises and Practice for Masterful Analysis of Others and Broadcasting of Yourself

In this section, you'll find several basic exercises to practice to enhance your analysis of others and influence over social interaction with deliberate communication. Select one or two you're comfortable with and start there. When you've become comfortable with those, select one or two more, and even add other practices you've found elsewhere and learned by observing others. Learning from others, you admire and then mirroring that behavior is an effective process of adapting a more influential behavior. The key is to practice them regularly and to record your results.

Regulate Your Breath

This is a common breathing technique used in meditation and in the practice of mindfulness. Like most breathing exercises, this is designed to guide the individual into a slower frame of mind that most often includes a slowing and calming of the body, as well. The individual is encouraged to listen to, and focus on, his or her own breath. When the mind wanders, gently guide it back to the breathing exercise.

This exercise can be practiced almost anywhere and at most times, but it does require the individual to block out the rest of the world for a solid 5-10 minutes for maximum benefit. There is no preparation necessary, and while it's nice to practice this exercise in a comfortable and relaxing space, it's possible to implement this in a space that isn't perfect. Doing so will actually only strengthen your resilience to block out distractions and concentrate deliberately for 5-10 minutes.

The primary function of this exercise is to regulate a slow, and steady breathing pattern of 3-count inhales, and 5-count exhales. It's also suggested than when breathing in, you breathe deeply through your nose, and when exhaling, you do so through the mouth as if you're blowing air out from your lips.

By adding this breathing exercise to your repertoire, you'll improve focus and memory and decrease stress chemicals in the body. This exercise also decreases the overall sense of anxiety, lowers heart rate and blood pressure, relieves muscle tension, and improves eyesight.

To practice this exercise:

Get as comfortable and quiet as possible where you can sit undisturbed for 5-10 minutes.

- Sit comfortably and close your eyes.
- Breathe in deeply as you normally would and exhale.
- Hold your breathing for a moment on the exhale.
- Inhale again, but this time, breathe in slowly and steadily for a count of 3 in your head.
- Hold your breath for a count of 3 in your head.
- Exhale, but this time, exhale in a slowly and steadily for a count of 5 in your head.
- Inhale again, slowly and steadily for a 3-count.

- Exhale again, slowly and steadily for a 5-count.
- Continue this pattern of slow and steady inhales and exhales at a 3-count, and 5-count, respectively.

You may opt to continue to hold your breath in between inhaling and exhaling as part of your pattern, but it's not mandatory. Do that which is most comfortable. If the mind begins to wander, gently bring it back to the observation of the breathing process. Your analytical mind should be listening closely to your breathing for any sign of faster or unsteady flow. The analytical mind can also remain focused on the evenness of your counts, trying to maintain the slow and steady flow. After a 5- or 10-minute period, you can slowly open your eyes and readjust to your immediate surroundings. With regular practice of this breathing exercise, you will teach your mind and body that you have the power to bring yourself to this peaceful moment whenever you want. This is a personal micro-vacation you can use any time in your day; it feels good.

Try Reframing

In reframing, you're encouraged to take a situation you feel negatively about, and put it in a new light; paint a different picture about it. This can be done anywhere, at any time, and takes only seconds or minutes. It can be done silently in your own mind, or out loud. Reframing out loud has the added benefit of strengthening the story, and the emotion of the story, to the subconscious mind with an additional auditory version of the story.

This exercise works well for individuals who regularly overthink, and form exaggerated and dramatic stories based on one small piece of evidence, often taken out of context. Examples of situations that reframing can work well on might be someone standing you up for a date, someone taking the seat you saved, someone cutting you off in the grocery aisle, a stranger giving you a nasty look, and so on. These situations often put us on the defensive quickly, as we feel we're wrongly judged or mistreated. It's easy to imagine a personal injustice or that the situation was done against you, personally.

In order to reduce this pattern of negative thoughts, and to practice positive thoughts, this exercise forces the individual to look at the situation objectively as if no personal emotion was involved. Through this lens, the individual can often slow the pattern of negative thought and put the situation into a more realistic perspective.

There are no step-by-step instructions for this practice. When you notice a situation, you feel personally offended by, stop. Take a moment to analyze what's really going on from an objective point of view. Ask yourself if you could be seeing some of these details wrong and if something else, which is not a personal attack on you, could actually be going on. Imagine a scenario in your mind, where the same situation plays out, but it has nothing to do with you. For example, the person who stood you up could have had an emergency. The person who took your seat probably didn't realize they did it. The person who cuts you off in the grocery aisle could have been in an important rush to get somewhere. The stranger with the nasty look could have made that face because of a thought of their own, and they just happened to be facing your direction.

Read Others in Public

The next time you're in any line, make a point to take your time reading and observing the body language of others around you; both customers and clerks. Note the correlations you observe, and even make notes on your phone about this while you're in line. Take time about once a month or once a quarter to look back over that which you've recorded to analyze your progress and the spots you still may need more work.

Exercise Written Influence

In-person interactions are a prime way to maximize influence, but this isn't always possible. Many times, we interact with others on the phone, in chat, or on social media. If email and text is the way you communicate for most of the day, try writing a persuasive email at least once per day. Plan what outcome you want to see and then try to implement one or two of these tactics to see if you can get the email recipient to do what you want or agree with you.

Try Listening

Listening can be perhaps the most important persuasion tactic you have in your tool kit. Listening to your prospect will give you most of the information you need for a successful persuasive conversation. By listening and paying careful attention to the words and body language, your prospect is communicating, and by listening carefully to the words they don't say, you'll be able to discern most of what you need.

There is still, however, information beyond that. By listening with deliberate intent, you make the prospect feel respected and understood. In some cases, this feeling is the most important part of the transaction.

By listening actively, you'll be able to ask thoughtful and insightful questions. Asking better questions will give the impression that you're already invested in delivering quality. Not only will the impression you make be appropriate, but you will actually gather crucial information that could influence the success of your interaction.

When listening is your primary technique, your prospects will notice this consciously or subconsciously, and they will want to listen to you and reciprocate that attention.

Listening isn't just hearing words; it requires an overall comprehension of the story being told. In many cases, individuals are not as clear and concise at expressing themselves, as you've become. So, listening to the conversation and finding the key components is up to you. Active listening also means paying attention to the sounds, tones, inflections, timbre, volume, and key used by the speaker. These details are also packed with information, revealing more insight into the speaker. By paying attention, you can determine someone's intentions, what they want you to think their intentions are, and what they expect of you.

If you have the opportunity, ask questions about the pieces that grabbed your curiosity, or that you're not clear about. This isn't just another opportunity to prove that you're a good listener; it's a prime time to ask questions that will draw out more information that you're seeking. This might mean asking your prospect questions that will cause them to express themselves in a certain way. You might be able to derive more insights from additional body language and other communicative behaviors. When you listen, acknowledge what's important to your prospect. See if you can determine the main argument and emotions.

Try Smiling

Your ability to smile is one of the most powerful tools to influence. This is true of influencing yourself or others. We've learned over thousands of years that the smile is a sign of happiness and friendship, so the smile helps to lower our defenses. When individual smiles, dozens of influential processes happen automatically.

For yourself, when you smile, you're releasing neurotransmitters like dopamine, and serotonin into your body, which benefits in a number of ways. The body relaxes automatically when you smile. This relaxation reduces heart rate, blood pressure, general pain, and general stress. A smile is so powerful that it can actually strengthen one's immune system and increase one's endurance as endorphins are released.

For others, a smile from you to them communicates positivity and happiness. For them, this is a subconscious reminder of the happiness of other smiles they've experienced and releases good feelings, cultivating a generally happier mood and disposition. It doesn't take much; even a smile that lasts but a millisecond packs enough power to affect those who see it. Recent studies suggest even exposure within a sixteenth of a millisecond is still powerful enough to have an influence on those who see it. The study exposed individuals to images of other people smiling, where exposure for 1/16th of a millisecond still influenced the group of individuals. Another set of individuals was exposed to images of people who were not smiling. At the end of the study, the participants were invited to all come to out to a venue for a complimentary night of music and free drinks. Those exposed to images of smiling people had more interactions, smiled more themselves, had more fun, and imbibed more drinks than those exposed to images of non-smiling people. Remember that while speaking in anger can be used to rouse feelings of aggression, this is not the influence you're looking for. A forced influence is a short-lived influence.

Try Vulnerability

It used to be so, in business as well as other aspects of life, showing that any sign of vulnerability was not good. To show vulnerability was to show weakness, leaving yourself open to attack and exploitation.

Today, that's not so much the case anymore. To display vulnerability, to a client or anyone, is the starting point for innovation and change. A bit of vulnerability, real or implied, makes the impression that you aren't afraid to face the music and you're accountable for what you say and do.

One way to demonstrate personal vulnerability is to be yourself. Often times, we hide a part of ourselves because we're worried about how it will be interpreted and what others will think. To be your true self puts you in a vulnerable spot. Others see this as bravery, and they subconsciously want to follow your lead and be themselves, too. They may not actually do it, but they at least reminded that they want to live bravely and be their true selves.

Try Empathy and Forgiveness

The ability to understand and related to another's feelings and experiences is yet another technique that can increase your powers of persuasion. If you want to use positive manipulation to drive interaction, it helps to know who you're working with. We like people who are like us, so if a prospect is sharing information with you, be empathetic. Doing so generates a sense of inclusion for your prospect, and that feeling of understanding and acceptance is your ticket to influencing an interaction.

Nod your head. Show concern. Show that you can relate to the stress or the happiness of a situation in the same way the prospect has reacted. All of this helps you to be more relatable to the prospect, which builds excellent rapport. The empathetic person has a much better chance of influencing a person or situation if reliability is already built into the rapport.

One of the key points of the empathetic approach is to capitalize on a perfect sense of timing. Sometimes a nod, a smile, an eyebrow raised, if done at the wrong time, can be distracting and off-putting for your prospect. Laughs and smiles, in particular, are important to get right. A misplaced laugh (or smile) amidst a devastating part of your prospect's story, is not going to build an empathetic rapport. It will build skepticism and distrust.

Practicing empathy means you'll have to put aside any feelings of superiority or pride. Where empathy puts you on the same playing field with your prospect, a sense of superiority will take you off again. You can't just try to cover up your sense of superiority; it's not about making sure the prospect doesn't see your attitude. If this is your frame of mind, you'll likely miss most of the details of communication.

Forgiveness is just as important as an ingredient, necessary for some kinds of conversation and communication. If a history of bad feelings has existed between two people or groups for a long time, forgiveness is sometimes the only act that can initiate a successful and beneficial breakdown of those old feelings.

Forgiveness has roots in the survival of our species. The act of forgiveness has, over thousands of years, helped to protect us. When we forgive someone, the benefit of that act is actually our own. It may feel nice to know about your subject that you forgive them and still accept them, but the relief you feel yourself when you forgive someone is tremendous. Letting go mentally and emotionally of the wrongs done to you is cleansing for you.

Forgiveness has also helped us, through the ages, to solidify an effective and efficient social structure within communities and groups. When an individual does something to go against a society's fundamental mores and customs, that individual is often subject to some version of shaming within the community. But forgiving the individual and letting them back into the group once the lesson has been learned is actually a very common way to practice unconditional love for group members. This practice can also strengthen one's loyalty to a group, for having been brought back into the group even after breaking fundamental social codes.

By practicing forgiveness, you build healthier relationships and improve your own mental health and state. Practicing forgiveness reduces the symptoms of depression and anxiety and improves heart health in the form of lowered blood pressure and heart rate. Knowing that you're strong enough to forgive someone can also generate feelings of accomplishment, capability, confidence, and strength. Self-esteem improves. All of these changes in the mental and emotional state are evident in the interaction, making you a calm and collected individual with the confidence and power to forgive. Your demeanor will echo this.

Try Silence

In many interactions that will cross your path, the best response is no response. The simple practice of staying silent can offer huge influence over an interaction. It can be a tricky practice because we're naturally so uncomfortable with extended silence within an interaction. But what you'll find is that when strategically timed and placed, silence in an interaction can be powerful leverage. The right silence can grab a listener's attention. The right silence can shake down your prospect and get them nervous about not taking your offer. The right silence can convey appreciation, anger, astonishment, confusion, or disapproval. Used at the right time and spot, the art of silence can convey many emotions and engage your prospect more, not less.

It's been said of debate and negotiation, that the individual to speak first is the one who loses. Holding your tongue in order to gather an ounce more information from your prospect gains you more leverage in the interaction. This is an early-taught tactic passed down from sales master to protégé. Business owners are privy to this tactic as well, as a defense against master sales vendors.

If someone makes you an offer, you can refuse. In fact, if it's the first offer, you should refuse. The idea here is to communicate to your prospect that you don't need the deal as badly as they do and that you're not afraid to walk away.

You can test this silent manipulation (in an innocuous and playful way) with one of your friends to see if you can influence them. The next time a friend suggests you get together, try the following and see what they do next:

Friend: Let's meet up for a basketball game this weekend.
You: A game, Hmmm.... (Silence)

Let your silence linger a bit longer than you normally would. Chances are your friend will be prompted to say something to justify the Meetup.

Friend: Yes, we haven't gotten together in a while.

Your silence will be a subconscious cue to your friend that you seem to be considering whether or not it's worth it to meet up. So, the next thing they say will be something to support or justify the idea of coming together. Not only will your friend be subconsciously aware that you might not find value in getting together for coffee, but your friend will also get a cue that you might not find them as valuable a friend. This will increase their nervousness of being rejected, and they'll be influenced by you to emphasize their worth. Obviously, this is an experiment you can test out which is short-lived and not harmful. Don't continue to repeat this over and over, however, or you may just lose your friends.

Similarly, to silence, consider using the whisper technique. Place a whisper strategically into the conversation in order to accentuate the call-to-action. By whispering to your audience or listener, you're creating a sense of secrecy and trust immediately. Not only is it an effective method for building rapport, but it sends a subliminal message about the urgency and discretion.

Practices to Maintain Balance

When you've spent much of your time learning to pay attention to minute details and microexpressions, your mind learns to look for and study the complex. It's important to take time to realign with other aspects of yourself. When the dynamic and complex has been your focus for too long, switch to a couple of minimalistic and simplifying practices. These suit the mind and the body, bringing about relaxation, peace, joy, comfort, lowered blood pressure and heart rate and a release of muscle pain. When your focus is so often in the details, take time to focus on one single and solitary thing- you.

Be Mindful of Yourself and Your Focus

Mindfulness, like simple living, is a concept that goes very far back through history but comes to the U.S. through relatively recently means. In the 1960s, the United States grew more familiar with Vietnamese Buddhist monk and activist, Thich Nhat Hanh. Hanh studied, practiced, and taught mindfulness, and in fact taught at Princeton and Columbia University in the 60s. It is primarily through the teachings of Thich Nhat Hanh that mindfulness has found its way into Western culture.

Thich Nhat Hanh taught in mindfulness to regularly take notice of where you are in your mental process.

He also taught the importance of slowing down to live in the moment and practice the small daily pieces of life with extra-sensory focus.

The teachings of Hanh were recognized by the American medical professor and society founder of the University of Massachusetts Medical School, Jon Kabat-Zinn. For a time, Kabat-Zinn was a student of Hanh's and eventually went on to develop the study of mindfulness as we know it today.

Many of the techniques and practices used today in coaching and therapy, as well as personal practice, are rooted in the same two concepts:

Bring yourself back. Refocus, recollect your thinking. When your mind begins to wander from the one thing you're doing, gently bring it back.

Savor the moment you're in right now. Rather than wanting to rush through one thing to get to another, appreciate the step you're at in this very moment. If you're washing the dishes, your mind should stay in the one dish you're washing. You pay extra close attention to the experience of washing this one particular plate in this one particular moment. If your mind starts to slip and think about the next plate you'll wash, you gently bring it back to the plate you're holding and focus on, quite literally, the task at hand.

Practicing mindfulness is a wonderful complement to practicing minimalism. Both remind the individual that simple is better. If it feels too complicated, you can probably simplify it, whether it's a physical space or a mental attitude. Here are a few mindfulness techniques commonly used by practitioners and therapists, as well as self-practicing individuals. Keep in mind they're all focused on the small and simple pieces of everyday life. They may seem mundane at first glance, but that's basically the point here. Something we might normally rush through is something we should fully observe and appreciate. That includes the moments that aren't so enjoyable.

Sit in a chair. Find a chair and sit in it. Don't do anything else. Sit in the chair only. Sit in that chair for about 5 minutes, and when your mind starts to wander, bring it back to the observation of the chair. How does it feel? How does it smell? What does it feel like? Hard or soft? Silky or leathery? What does your skin feel like on the chair? What does it sound like when you move in the chair? And when your mind begins to wander, gently bring it back to focus on the experience of sitting in a chair, and nothing else.

Eat mindfully. When you're eating, alone or in a group, at home or at the office, in any situation you find yourself eating practice mindfulness. Move your utensils more slowly than you normally might. Take a bite on your fork or spoon that will easily fit into your mouth without a struggle. Chew that piece of food more slowly than you normally might. Pay closer attention to the textures and flavors. Put your utensil down while you chew. Take a sip of water after swallowing your food.

Engage the senses. This can be something as simple as enjoying the smell of the soap or shampoo you use in the shower, or something as extreme as skydiving. There's a wide range of activities from one to the other, and you're sure to find comfort somewhere between them. Give your senses a new thrill. Visit a new city or town. Listen to new music. Rent a car just to switch it up. Try a food you've never had. Find ways of igniting the senses.

Listen, and nothing else. When someone is talking, give your full attention to them. Be attentive to the language they use to express themselves. Pay attention to their body language and what they don't say. If you're on the phone with someone, sit down and talk to them as if they were in front of you. Avoid talking on the phone while you're doing ten other things around your house.

Do not multitask. Get it yet? It's about doing one thing, and one thing only, and dedicating your focus and attention to that one thing until it's complete. As often as you can, practice giving your full attention to one process at a time and watch how much faster you excel at the activity.

Learn from pain. It's part of life. There's bound to be some discomfort. If you want flowers, you've got to have showers. Mindfulness says to be patient and kind with yourself about that, too. In the moments of life that don't necessarily feel good subjectively, you can still experience calm and happiness in knowing that you will learn and grow from this painful experience.

The primary benefit of practicing mindfulness is giving the analytical mind something to do and focus on; observe the moment, savor the moment. The busy analytical mind has an activity to engage in, which keeps the mind from otherwise following the negative streams of thought to a sad conclusion.

The secondary benefit of practicing mindfulness is the natural increase in positivity. By practicing mindfulness, individuals often gain satisfaction from the realization that they could enjoy doing things much more when the goal is simply to enjoy doing anything that comes to them.

In addition to these rather abstract benefits, the practice of mindfulness can benefit in physical, measurable ways, too. Mindfulness often helps to lower heart rate and blood pressure, increase circulation, release tense muscles and joints, and assists in helping sick individuals to recover faster.

Take Some Time to Stop the Thought

Meditation is an ancient practice that dates back as early as 5000BC, and perhaps even further. Thus, it's difficult to say with any accuracy when and where meditation began. What's easily known is that meditation began to make its way into the United States at the end of the 1800s, as the western world became familiar with India through Great Britain. At a time in society when the paranormal and the occult were all the rage, meditation, and really any exotic alternative that broke norms and challenged taboos, fit right in.

Meditation on a large scale can represent a religious devotion. Meditation on a smaller scale can offer a decrease in perceptual stress and anxiety, and improved health, especially of the heart and circulatory system. It's recommended that you meditate for as little as 10 minutes each day. Meditating for a longer period of time can be beneficial too, but for many, it creates too much resistance, and only 10-20 minutes is achievable. A routine practice of 10 minutes or more, at least once a day, can have a significant impact on you physically and mentally.

There are many people who think meditation doesn't work for them, or they cannot do it. This is an unfortunate misconception. In almost every case of this, the individual has been misinformed about what meditation is, and what's to be expected. When the individual is freed from the restrictive thoughts of what meditation must be, they are able to enjoy its benefits without resistance.

There are many different types of meditation, but in one form or another, most forms of meditation focus on creating a silence in mind. In whichever form of meditation, you practice, this usually means that you become quiet and still and focus on an external stimulus like the sound of your breathing or the sound of the wind or water. When your mind begins to wander, you bring it back to the moment and refocus on the sound of your breath, or the wind, or the water.

Let's take a look at several types of meditation that can be easily practiced almost anywhere, by almost anyone. Pay attention to which forms of meditation sound comfortable to you and test one out today.

Good Intentions Meditation: In this meditation exercise, you sit in a peaceful and quiet location for about 10 minutes with your eyes closed. During this time, you keep your mind on only one thought. The thought is usually a message of loving-kindness you want to send to someone. For example, let's say a friend has a broken leg and you're hoping for them to recover soon. To perform a kindness meditation, prepare a short basic sentence that expresses your love for your friend and your desire to see them well again. As you meditate, repeat this phrase as a sort of mantra, all the while trying to elicit the positive emotional feelings of seeing your friend well again. When the mind wanders, bring it back to this mantra.

Progressive Relaxation: In this meditation exercise, you sit in a calm and quiet environment and become still and soft. Typically, you would begin by slowing the breath and listening to it; concentrating on the sound of it. After about a minute or so, you focus on one small aspect of your being with the goal of relaxing it. For example, let's say it's time to relax your jaw. Wiggle your jaw and stretch it out for a moment. Imagine the tiny muscles and nerves in your chin relaxing. Imagine your tongue relaxing. Move your tongue around in your mouth, and feel it relax. As you relax each part, you move to another, slowly relaxing pieces of yourself from head to toe. If you intend to practice meditation for longer than 10 minutes, this is an excellent one to start with. It keeps the analytical mind focused on the task, and the extra relaxation makes it easy to stay in this meditation for upwards of 20 minutes.

Breathing Exercises: There are many different breathing exercises that work effectively, and the key is to find one or two that you really like to use. In a breathing meditation, the main objective is to only focus on the sounds and feelings of your own breath. When the mind wanders to other thoughts, it returns to the breath. One very common breathing exercise is to close your eyes and breathe in and out slowly and comfortably. As you inhale, count to 3. Hold your breath in your lungs for a moment and then exhale and count to 5 so that your exhale is slightly longer. Focus on this practice only for 10 minutes. Another popular breathing exercise is to breathe slow and deep and when you do, imagine that breath going into a sore or uncomfortable area of the body; a sore back perhaps. You imagine that breath stretching out the sore area and giving it a good massage, and as you exhale, you imagine the soreness leaving with your breath.

Stretching and Breathing: This yoga practice doubles as a meditation practice and the individual experiences peace of mind through focus, and physical health benefits as well. To practice Kundalini, you would learn a set of poses or movements that you would blend together. Each time you restart the movements, you focus on making them as perfect as you can. When the mind wanders, you bring it back to your form. The set of movements usually includes 4 - 8 poses that start over at the completion of each set.

There are of course many other forms of meditation, and if none of these sound as if they'll suit you, don't give up on meditation. Consider what it is you're looking for in an effective meditative exercise and then use other resources to find the form of meditation that will best suit you.

By adding as little as 10 minutes of meditation to your day, you're reducing stress and anxiety. You're quieting the mind and training it to know that obsessive negative thought patterns are not the only thought patterns you have at your disposal. Giving yourself the opportunity to rest the body and mind simultaneously for just 10 minutes a day promotes emotional health and enhances self-worth and self-actualization.

Meditation is an excellent tool for lengthening the attention span and improving memory, and it can actually reduce memory loss for seniors as they age. You can look forward to more control over your thoughts and emotions with 10 minutes to realign and focus.

Conclusion

Congratulations! You've made it to the end of *How to Analyze People: The Complete Guide to Read Nonverbal Communication, Apply Emotional Intelligence, and Detect Lying.*

The power of influence, manipulation, and seduction is now a topic that you can make sense of, and with which you no longer need to feel alienated or broken. You understand what positive influence really means, and how to use it in conjunction with other deliberate practices for maximum results. You've also learned what to watch out for in terms of negative manipulation going on around you and focused toward you.

What's more, you've completed the initial, crucial, steps to read others, and influence interactions of a social, business, or romantic flavor. As you've worked through these chapters, you've expanded your knowledge on the history of manipulation and how it also plays a part in today's media. You're now more aware of professionals who constantly rely on these applications for their own success. Hopefully, you've gained insight, confidence, and practical application from the information in this book.

Not only have you become familiar with the practices it takes to become an excellent reader of others' body language and vocal communications, but you've also learned that positive and deliberate persuasion can help you to repair existing relationships that may be experiencing strain.

When your life feels out of your control, you can change the direction with deliberate influence. When you slip up or forget what to do, the exercises in this book will set you back on point and help you to get down to the nitty-gritty positive work once again. You're encouraged to continue regularly practicing with the wealth of knowledge you now have, and to expand your knowledge and evolve yet again.

Practical and ethical influence and manipulation will take you a long way. With this information in this book, you're ready to stop bending to the wills of others are start implementing the life and future you want with persuasion tactics.

Printed in Great Britain
by Amazon

57991083R00092